Image of God

From Who You Are To Who You Can Become

By

Jeff Crawford

Image of God
From Who You Are To Who You Can Become
by Jeff Crawford

Printed in the United States of America

ISBN 978-1-60647-921-6

www.xulonpress.com

For Julie,
It is not good that man should be alone, so
God sent you to me.

Table of Contents

Introduction – The Image of God

This is a book about *you*. But first let me tell you a little bit about me.

I am 39 years old.
I have three kids.
I am six feet tall.
I love sci-fi movies.
I collect comic books.
I have brown hair.
I hate lima beans.
I drive a blue Ford pick-up.
I have a hot wife.
I am a Christian.

Based on who you are, where you come from, and how you define yourself, you will already have formed some kind of opinion about who you think I am. But here's the deal: apart from the little information I have given you above, you really don't know me at all. You may think you do, but you don't. Yet in just 45 words, you have formed some kind of picture in your mind, either positive or negative, about me.

Who we are as people is so much more complex than a mere 45 words, or 45 pages, or 45 chapters could ever describe. In fact, if you could actually meet me for just 45 seconds, your entire *image* of me would be altered. Even then you wouldn't know me completely.

The truth is, as human beings, we are immensely complex. So complex that we struggle to even figure out ourselves. I'm still trying to decide what I want to be when I grow up! People really do want to know who they are as individuals. For many, it is a life-long pursuit to answer the BIG questions that dog us.

Where did I come from?

Who am I, really?

What is wrong with me?

How do I fix it?

These four questions, I believe, are at the crux of the human struggle for understanding and significance.

We are in love with ourselves. Go into any bookstore, even a Christian bookstore, and you will see a plethora of material on *you*. It's as if we can't get enough of ourselves. No matter how many books we read or how many episodes of Oprah we watch, the questions remain and the search goes on.

That brings me to this book. In many ways, the book you are holding has grown out of my own personal search for the answers to the four questions listed above. Believe it or not, I think I've found them. Oh, I am not claiming to have it all figured out, by any means. My search to understand God and myself is still ongoing. In fact, I believe it will continue until I die. But I am convinced I have found the right track to run on, so I want to share with you what I have found.

This book is about you. And it is about me. It is about all of us who fit into the category of "mankind." It doesn't matter if you are tall or short. Whether you are American, or European, or African, or Lebanese. Color of skin is irrelevant. Economic status and education level are don't matter. Whoever you are, this book is very simply about *you*.

What makes this book different is that our search into the essence of what it means to be human will be drawn squarely from the Bible. These aren't just my random thoughts. The Bible is my textbook. In fact, the Bible is *also* a book about you. I would even go as far as to say that this book you are holding right now would make an excellent study guide to go right alongside your Bible. If you don't own a Bible, I highly recommend you go buy one because along the way you will find yourself wanting to go to the source material yourself.

The Bible is where our journey begins. In the very first chapter of the Bible we see God at work doing one of the things He loves best: creating. God loves to create and we see Him in Genesis working on His masterpiece. He places the stars in space. He forms the earth out of nothingness. Plants, sea life, and land animals are all painted into existence.

Then, in verse 26 of that first chapter, we see the crowning act of God's creation:

"Let us make man in our image, after our likeness."

This is a fascinating declaration, so easily read over, too quickly passed by. We see that mankind is *different* from all the rest of God's creation. All of creation is just simply spoken into existence. But there is something more at work when God speaks Man into existence, and I am sure you are already ahead of me on this one. Man was created in the "Image of God." We were created after God's *likeness*. This is a radical shift from all the rest of God's creation. It makes us unique in God's story. God is up to something.

So, in just nine words, we have the answer to two of our four big questions. Where did you come from? God. Who are you? You are the Image of God. It's probably hard for you to wrap your mind around that second answer. It is for me as well. Yet it is true. Despite all of our differences as people, we really *are* all the same. You, me, us, we have all been created in the Image of God.

What exactly does it mean that you are the Image of God? That is what I will address and examine in the bulk of this book. But let me say a word here about what it does *not* mean.

Being the Image of God does not mean that you are a god. Polytheism is the belief in multiple gods. The word *poly* means many and the word *theos* means god. It is not uncommon to encounter people in our increasingly spiritualized culture who believe in the existence of many gods. Hinduism fits into this category with the claim that there are over 330 million gods. Other religious groups even claim that Man has the capacity to become a god himself. This is a mainstay belief of the Church of Jesus Christ of Latter Day Saints, the Mormons. None of this is what the Bible means when it says that you are the Image of God. There is only *one* God.

Notice that when God makes His declaration of the creation of Man, He uses the word *us.* "Let us make man...." Who is us? How can God be *one* and be *us*? What we see here is not polytheism, but instead the beginning of the revelation that God is a Trinity. One God in three Persons. It is not within the scope of this book to explore this critical belief of orthodox Christianity, but for practical purposes, think of H^2O. What is H^2O? Your first response is probably water. But what if I freeze it? What if I boil it? Water, ice, steam. Three radically different expressions of the same substance: H^2O. This is one way to think about God as Trinity. One God expressed in three distinct persons, each with a unique function: Father, Son, Holy Spirit.

Being the Image of God does not mean that you are god. Pantheism is the belief that everything is a part of god. The word *pan* means all. The trees, the birds, the chair, you: all god. This is a common theme in much of New Age spirituality. Who can forget Shirley MacLaine standing on a beach loudly exclaiming, "I am god!" in the 1987 film *Out on a Limb*? Pantheism is popular because it puts Man in the driver's seat. You can create your own morality and there is no accountability. But just as is the case with polytheism, this is not what it means to be the Image of God. As I have stated and as the Bible expresses, there is only one God. His creation is not to be confused with Him as the Creator. That includes you and me as well. We are the *Image* of God, we are not god.

The Bible uses two words in Genesis 1:26 to describe you as a creation of God. Those two words are *image* and *likeness*. They are two different words in the Hebrew language as well as in English. Both words mean essentially the same thing. They could be translated *resemblance* or *model*. Think about that. You are not God, but He made you to *resemble* Him. You have been *modeled* after God. How cool is that?

Last year my son Garrett and I took over the dining room table for about two weeks as we put together a model of Jeff Gordon's #24 DuPont Chevrolet. We've become NASCAR fans around my house in the last couple of years. My wife and I were looking for something to fill the gap between football seasons each year and neither basketball nor baseball was cutting it for us. Something about NASCAR just fit. Needless to say, our kids caught the fever as well, and with Jeff Gordon's super hot streak of six wins (twice winning back-to-back) in the 2007 season, Garrett wanted to build his car for display in his room.

I was on board, so we went down to *Hobby Lobby* and bought the Jeff Gordon #24 model. When we opened the box, it was just a mish-mash of plastic pieces and a sheet of decals. It looked nothing like the fire red and metallic blue signature

Chevy driven by Gordon. But everything we needed was in the box. That is key. Don't miss it. We had everything we needed in the box, it just had to be put together.

It was a daunting task. I was impressed with the detail. The first page of instructions was just for the engine. I couldn't believe how much of the model was given to portions of the car that you would never see once it was put together. That's the point of the model – accuracy. An authentic *resemblance* of the real thing. After two weeks of working, we were almost there. The last step after all the glue and the paint was applying the decals. I hate decals. Remember the decals from your model kits when you were a kid? They haven't changed. We can put a man on the moon, but we can't make decals easy. Amazing. And the decals are critical. It's what everyone will see. You mess up here and the image falls apart. You end up with the #24 car after it's rubbed the wall at Talladega, or tangled with Tony Stewart's #20 car. Not a pretty sight.

But we did it. If you go into my son's room today and look on his shelf, you will see the image of Jeff Gordon's #24 DuPont Chevrolet. If you look inside, you'll even see the image of Jeff himself! But it's not Jeff, and it's not his car. Far from the real thing, it is an image. A resemblance. A model.

This is a good way to describe you. God created you in His image. It is a wonderful, awesome and holy thing. But life is hard. There are walls and other cars that get in the way. You may have even found yourself looking in the mirror and wondering exactly where the Image of God is in all that mess. Listen, we've all been there, are there. But let me assure you that everything you need is still in the box. You may need to go back to the Maker's body shop and let Him work on you. That is where I hope this book will come in handy.

This book is presented to you as a story, or drama. There are two acts and an intermission. Act 1 describes our current condition as the disfigured Image of God. I will show you how this happened and all the implications of our disfigurement for everyday life. Then there is an Intermission. Intermissions are designed to give you a break from the story, go to the rest room, get something to drink, but mostly to let the events of Act 1 set in and to then prepare for Act 2. The intermission is important, even critical. Thus is the case with the intermission in the drama of this book. Don't miss the intermission because it will pave the way for you to join the story in Act 2.

In the last half of the book, I will show you what the restored Image of God can look like in your life. This requires participation. This is where the book can become a manual of sorts to help you recover the Image of God in your own life. You must participate in the Intermission for this to happen; otherwise you will be stuck forever in Act 1.

Shall we begin?

The curtain is about to rise.

ACT 1 – The Image of God

Disfigured

Chapter 1 – Sinner

Sin is not a popular word today. It smacks of judgmentalism, close-mindedness, intolerance. Our secular culture glories in free thinking, freedom of speech and freedom of expression. We love our freedom! Sin just sort of comes along and takes all the fun out of our freedom party, doesn't it? Now imagine actually calling someone a *sinner*. It just doesn't fly. We are so politically correct these days that you can't call a spade a spade. I find it humorous how politicians challenge each other. If one candidate lies about another candidate or about his own record, the other side will never say they *lied*. They, instead, will use the subtle language of "they misspoke," or "they misrepresented the facts." They will never call their opponent a liar, even if they are one. We just can't bring ourselves to do that. We can't even bring ourselves to look in the mirror and honestly evaluate our own self.

A 2008 survey by Ellison Research in Phoenix, Arizona reveals some interesting information about how we view sin. The survey defines sin as "something that is almost always considered wrong, particularly from a religious or moral perspective." It found, according to this definition of sin, that 87% of people believe that sin does indeed exist. When pressed on what actually is a sin, some of the biggies get called out: 81% called adultery a sin and 73% called racism a sin. But other sins get a pass in terms of majority opinion, such as premarital sex and gambling. What is even more striking is the attitude people hold toward sin's effects on them personally. While the overwhelming majority of people believe in sin, it doesn't appear that they view themselves as sinners. Most people, 65%, believe that they are headed for heaven. What is really shocking, but maybe not, is that only .05% of the people surveyed think they are going to hell. Either people don't view themselves as sinners or they just don't think that sin makes a difference on someone's, especially their own, eternal destiny. While the survey didn't go in this direction, it is also possible that some of the people who participated in the survey don't even believe in a heaven or a hell. At the end of the survey, we are left with more questions than answers. What exactly is a sin? And what isn't a sin? Who sins? And does sin make any difference at all in my life?

Here is the truth, and listen to me carefully: You *are* a sinner. And so am I. Whew! Now that we have that out of the way we can move on. I am going to admit that this is a very risky way to begin a book. And in chapter 1, no less. I'm telling you that sin is just not "in," and we don't want to think about it, much less read about it. So my risk is high. I risk you turning me off before you even turn the page. I risk you throwing me into some sort of stereotype preacher category who loves to brow-beat people with hell, fire, and brimstone. Someone who loves to point a finger at others and nit-pick all the sin in their lives and talk about how God is going to judge them.

The truth is, I'm really not like that at all. I love people and tend to see the best in them and not the worst. I tend to want to give people the benefit of the doubt. I tend to see people for who they can be and not who they are. I have dedicated my life to teaching and preaching to those who are already in the camp, while at the same time making the message of Christ accessible to those who aren't in yet (and by the way, there's a bunch of sin both inside and outside the camp). I am definitely pro-people. Since this book is about people, and more specifically about you, I have to be honest and start at the beginning. The beginning for us is the beginning of God's story in the Bible. The book of Genesis. In the beginning there was God. And there was light. And there was creation. And there was, unfortunately, sin.

That is where we start. Like it or not. But I promise you this: we may start low, but we won't stay here. The book gets better, I promise. So stick with me, okay? I do warn you, this book is not for those who want to play around with life. This is a very serious book about a serious topic…you. If *you* are serious about *you* and truly do want to learn about who you are, why you are here, and where you are going, then this is the book not only *about* you, but *for* you.

The Image Marred

So there they were.
Adam and Eve.
Male and female.
Husband and wife.
In the Garden of Eden.
Paradise on earth.

The Image of God in flesh and blood. Could it get any better? But then something happened, something went horribly wrong. The Image of God became disfigured.

It is difficult to overstate the tragic events of that day recorded in the third chapter of Genesis. Adam and Eve were living in perfect unity. The Image of God, both male and female, was intact and in unison. The Bible declares that they "were both naked and were not ashamed" (Genesis 2:25). We read so easily past that verse but it deserves a pause.

I have been married 16 years to a woman that is God's precious gift to me. Without her, I am not complete. It was not good that Jeff should be alone, so God brought Julie "unto" me. Just like when Adam saw Eve, when I first saw Julie Dickson, I said, "Woe – man!" (some of you will get that later). We dated, fell in love, and eventually got married. The two became one flesh. When Julie and I are functioning the way we should, in pure selfless love, we are an expression of the Image of God. Our sexual intimacy is a picture of that image operating in perfect unity. We are together, we are naked, and we are not ashamed. But let me tell you that it is not always that way. You see, I am a sinner. I mess up. I, more times than I want to admit, put *me* first. When I sin and put myself ahead of my wife, let me tell you brother, the clothes ain't comin' off! We may be together, but the clothes are definitely on and we are ashamed. Some of you know exactly what I mean.

Adam and Eve, in the Garden of Eden, lived in perfect selfless unity. In fact, the Garden of Eden was the first nudist colony because Adam and Eve walked around the whole time naked! The thought of clothing was foreign to them. If it got cold, well....you know. I say all this tongue and cheek, but I think you get the point. There was a pure innocence in the Garden *because* Adam and Eve were one flesh reflecting perfectly the Image of God. This is foreign to us today because we have nothing we can compare this to other than the words of Genesis.

Snakes, Trees, and Rules

Immediately after those incredible words at the end of chapter two, our story takes an ominous turn in the first three words of chapter 3, "Now the serpent..." Listen, when snakes show up, it's *never* good. And when snakes start to talk, like in a Disney movie come to life, it's only going to get worse. I am not going to pretend to understand all the ins and outs of what took place next, but the Bible records that Satan appeared to Eve in the form of a snake and began a conversation. Maybe since the rules of man / animal relations were different in the Garden, it wasn't a big deal for Eve to be having a conversation with a snake. Needless to say, the whole incident speaks to the power of Satan to deceive (we will go much deeper into Satan's involvement with us as the Image of God in chapter 5).

The conversation that Satan engaged Eve in surrounds a tree and a rule. There was one special tree in the center of the Garden called the Tree of the Knowledge of Good and Evil. There was one rule of conduct that God gave Adam and Eve: don't eat the fruit from *that* tree.

Here is what is interesting about this one rule: God gave the rule specifically to Adam, not to Adam *and* Eve. In fact, Eve had not been created by God at the time the rule was issued (Genesis 2:15-16). God gave the rule to Adam, and he expected that Adam would teach this rule to his wife and his children. He expected that this one rule would be passed down through the generations.

Sounds simple, huh? Don't you wish *you* only had one rule to follow in life? How could Adam blow it? But before you come down too hard on Adam, let's just consider this one rule thing for a minute. Guys, what if God spoke to you tomorrow and exempted you from all the laws in the Bible? All the do's and don'ts no longer apply to you. Except for one. What if God said that the only thing he wanted you to do was not look upon a woman and lust? That's it. Only one rule. How long do you think you'd make it? Ladies, what if God only gave you one rule to follow? Just one. What if God told you that the only thing He expected out of you was to never harbor feelings of bitterness? That's it. Only this one rule. How long do you think you could last?

How long did Adam and Eve last? The Bible doesn't tell us, but I believe it wasn't very long. In fact, I think it was less than nine months. You see, at the time that the snake began his conversation with Eve, there were no children yet. Nine months is not very long, is it? Especially when you only have one rule to follow. But I'm not sure any of us would last nine months, or even nine days for that matter. The point is, it doesn't matter what the rule or rules are, Satan will attack, his attack will be subtle, and it will be very deceptive. So deceptive that we will convince ourselves that we aren't breaking a rule at all. *"Sinner? Not me. I'm not a sinner...."*

Adam's Sin

At this point in our story, it is easy to put the blame on Eve. After all, the snake is talking to her and not to Adam. They are having a very deep conversation about the tree and about the rule. The snake questions whether or not Eve has heard the rule correctly.

> *He said to the woman, "Did God actually say, 'You shall not eat of any tree in the garden'?"[1]*

Then the snake questions the punishment that God has promised for breaking this one rule. You see, God was very clear. He told Adam that he would die the very day he broke this rule (Genesis 2:17). This rule business is serious business. One rule. You break it, you die.

There are those who believe that God wasn't really talking about physical death when he laid out what the punishment would be for Adam and Eve if they ate from the Tree of the Knowledge of Good and Evil. They point out that Adam and Eve did not, in fact, die. They insist that what God was talking about as a punishment was a spiritual

24

death. Some have even suggested that Adam and Eve would have lived forever in the Garden, but that God's punishment was mortality. Since they ate the fruit, Adam and Eve would begin to age and eventually die.

Now I certainly believe that Adam and Eve did experience a spiritual death, and it may be true that as a result of breaking the rule they became mere mortals. But I do not believe that explanation is anywhere close to what God meant when He said they would die. I believe, and I believe that Adam believed, that God meant what He said. On the very day that Adam ate that fruit, he would die. As in dead. The Hebrew word here in Genesis 2:17 is *"mooth."* It is a powerful word used over 800 times in the Bible and it means most literally "dead," "death," or even "kill." It is a word used to describe violent, physical death. To read this verse any other way is to gloss over the seriousness that God took toward His one rule.

As we look back at this scene where Eve and the snake are discussing God's tree and God's rule, there is something, or someone, glaringly missing.

Adam.

Where's Adam? God gave the rule to Adam to give to Eve. She is his responsibility. So often, Eve takes the rap for what happened in Eden on that fateful day. After all, she's the one that entertained a conversation with a snake, she's the one who eventually messed up....first. But that is not the way I see it at all. I want to know where Adam was. Did he impress upon Eve the importance of the rule? Was he watching over her in the manner that a husband is to watch over his wife? They were "one flesh" after all.

If someone were to ask me what the first sin ever committed was, I would not say that it was the eating of the fruit from the Tree of the Knowledge of Good and Evil. I would say that the first sin ever committed was Adam's sin. His sin of selfishness. Somehow, in some way, on some level,

I believe that the Bible is showing us, by way of Adam's absence, that he failed in his responsibilities toward his wife and he put *self* first. Adam's sin was putting Adam first.

Here's something I have learned about sin: It never operates in isolation. Adam's sin of self first led to his sin of neglect. Neglect of his wife, Eve. This sin of neglect led to Eve finding herself in a compromising position out from under the protective care of her husband. As a result, she was vulnerable. She fell prey to her own sin: Independence from Adam. In a very real way, she put herself first when she finally succumbed to the snake's suggestion and picked and ate the fruit. She was saying, "I don't care what Adam says about this silly rule. I don't care what God says about the rule. What kind of rule is this anyway? I *want* to eat the fruit and I *will* eat the fruit."

And she did.

And he did.

And the proverbial snowball began to roll down the hill.

Lucifer's Sin

Before we move on with the story of the first human sin, let's look just for a moment at the snake. As mentioned previously, the snake was an incarnation of Satan.

Have you ever wondered where Satan came from? How did this being we call Satan become "Satan?" The word "Satan" means "the accuser." He is the devil, the destroyer, the accuser. That is exactly what he did in the Garden with Eve. He accused Eve of not understanding God. He accused God of being dishonest with Adam and Eve. As a result, he succeeded in destroying what Adam and Eve shared in the Garden.

But where did Satan come from and what was *his* sin? Before he was Satan he was Lucifer, one of the most striking and beautiful angels in heaven. He was called "an anointed guardian cherub" (Ezekiel 28:14). It is possible that before the foundations of the earth were laid, he was in charge of "guarding" heaven. From what? We don't know, but isn't it interesting that if this is true, that Satan once guarded heaven, he would know exactly how to attack it?

As Lucifer, he was one of God's chief angels. Some theologians believe that Lucifer occupied the office of archangel. It is also believed that at any given time there is only one archangel in God's army of heavenly hosts. When Lucifer surrendered this position, he was replaced by the current archangel, Michael. This was Lucifer, the Day Star, the supreme angel, God's right-hand man, so to speak.

Why did Lucifer give up such an important and exalted position in heaven? What could be better than serving God? We are given a clue in the book of Isaiah.

> *"How you are fallen from heaven, O Day Star, son of Dawn! How you are cut down to the ground, you who laid the nations low! You said in your heart, 'I will ascend to heaven; above the stars of God I will set my throne on high; I will sit on the mount of assembly in the far reaches of the north; I will ascend above the heights of the clouds; I will make myself like the Most High.'*
>
> *But you are brought down to Sheol, to the far reaches of the pit.*[2]

In this fascinating passage we are able to pull back the veil and peer into the mind of Lucifer, soon to be Satan. We are able to see the mind of evil being born.

The passage begins with a lament over the fall of heaven's star, the great Lucifer. Then the passage shifts to the mind of Lucifer and we see him quoted. We see five statements, each expressing a desire to be higher than God, to sit on God's throne. We see his hunger for power spring forth as he wants to seize control of God's creation. He proclaims that he will be like God and even above and greater than God. It is the ultimate self-deception.

Look carefully at the five statements of Lucifer and you will see a common thread. In them you see Lucifer's sin and perhaps the first sin committed in all of God's creation. Each statement begins with the same two words, "I will...."

I will...

I *will*...

I will...

I WILL...

I WILL...!!

Five expressions of Lucifer's will, not God's will. What was it that turned Lucifer into Satan? What was it that caused him to fall from heaven, to become the accuser and the destroyer? What was Lucifer's sin? His *will*. The sin of me. Self. Selfishness. Pride. Call it what you will, but the path of Lucifer is the same path that Adam found himself walking. It is the same path of destruction that the Destroyer led Eve down. The path of *me*.

Nuclear Fallout

The ultimate fear for many people in our world is nuclear conflict. The power of a nuclear bomb is almost indescribable. One ten-kiloton nuclear bomb detonated in our nation's capital would destroy everything in its path for a half of a mile. The fallout would contaminate everything in a 3,000 to 5,000 square-mile radius. The human toll would make 9/11 look like a small incident. Over 300,000 people would die within minutes.[3] In addition, the entire infrastructure of the whole region would be wiped out. The electromagnetic pulse generated by the blast would fry cell phone, radios, televisions and anything electronic. Life as we know it would come to a grinding halt.[4]

The fallout from a nuclear blast goes far beyond the initial days, weeks and months of detonation. On August 6, 1945, the United States of America dropped an atomic bomb on Hiroshima. The blast affected the ecosystem, unleashing a torrent of "black rain" upon the survivors. This radioactive black rain had an impact that affected genetic reproduction for a generation. The result was thousands of birth defects, and children with severe mutations. The cost of the blast on that August day can still be felt today.

The first sin, the sin of me, has had its own nuclear fallout. You see, this is an attribute of sin, its effects are never isolated, and the repercussions can last more than a generation. As much as we would like it to, sin never exists in a vacuum. There will be continued consequences for us, our friends, our family, for strangers, for everyone.

Adam and Eve break God's rule. Their selfishness leads them to nuclear detonation. Look at what happens immediately to them. The story records that "the eyes of both of them were opened, and they knew that they were naked (Genesis 3:7)." Can you believe it? The concept of "naked" occurs to Adam and Eve for the first time. What do they do now? They start grabbing leaves and vegetation to cover themselves up! Question...who's going to see them? They're the only two people on earth. They've already seen what the other one's got. What's the big deal? The big deal is sin. I think it is important to note that the very first, and immediate, result of their sin is a barrier erected between husband and wife. You see, that's what sin does. It destroys the intimacy of marriage. It breaks fellowship. It ruins relationships. The Image of God has taken a severe blow. It has become marred and disfigured.

Now for the fallout. The very next thing that happens in our story is that God comes looking for them. Uh oh, Adam and Eve hear footsteps in the Garden. God is coming. They've been caught. What do they do? What does any kid do when Dad comes looking for him because he did something wrong? Hide. Adam and Eve run for cover. This one "little" sin has not only divided a husband and wife, it has now severed Man's relationship with God. Let me say it again: Sin destroys relationships.

Can a man run from God? Getting back to our story, God wants to know what's going on, so He seeks out Adam and Eve, confronting them with their sin. That's another thing about sin. You can't run from it. You can try. You can lie and run and cheat and do all kinds of things to cover your sin, but in the end, your sin will find you. God will find you. Remember, 87% of people are convinced that sin does indeed exist.

God confronts the couple with their sin. This is the first marriage counseling session in the history of the world. Look at how it goes. As in so many marriages, Adam and Eve start the blame game. Adam refuses to take ownership for his sin. He blames Eve. "It's that woman, that *you* gave me, God. It's all *her* fault!" Can you believe it? Adam blames Eve and God for his sin. Eve will have none of it. She points the finger at the snake. "It's *his* fault, he deceived me." So much is said today about our victim culture. People rarely take responsibility for their own actions anymore. It's always someone else's fault. The truth is that the blame culture has been in full swing since the Garden of Eden. It is part of the nuclear fallout of sin.

These are the immediate consequences of sin's detonation. Broken relationships within marriage and with God. But the ripple effects have only begun in our story. God lays out additional consequences. To the woman: Pain during childbirth and contempt for her husband will mark who she is. New life will HURT, and she will have a spirit that will seek to supplant the God-given role of her husband as her head. God is saying that marriage will be hard. She will have to work at it. The reward won't come easy. To the man:

No more free ride. No more lazy days in the Garden eating grapes and letting the animals bring food to him while he lays on his bed of palm leaves. Now he has to work. It takes sweat, blood and tears, just to get clean water to drink and food to grow. He will be at the mercy of the weather. There will be good seasons and bad seasons. It will be like this until he breathes his last breath. Nuclear fallout.

There's more. Here is where you and I come in. Because of Adam's one sin, his DNA took a blow. It was changed, deformed. Sin became part of the human condition. Theologians call this Original Sin, or Sin Nature. Basically, the nuclear fallout of sin changed what it means to be human. In a very literal sense, the spiritual DNA of Adam was mutated in such a way that he passed down to future generations, all the way to us today, this inclination to sin. There is nothing we can do about it.

I have brown eyes because my dad has brown eyes. All three of my children have brown eyes because of me and because of my dad. It is a trait that we Crawfords pass down. There was nothing I could do about it and there was nothing my children could do about it. You can't fight your genes. In the same way, this sin "gene" comes to us all and we can no more avoid it than I can my brown eyes. Sin is the black rain that mutates the soul.

Therefore, just as sin came into the world through
one man, and death through sin, and so death spread
to all men because all sinned – [5]

When Heroes Sin

It's a tough thing when a hero falls. As a kid, I had all sorts of heroes. My favorite was Iron Man. Oh, sure, I loved Spider Man, X-men, and Superman. Didn't everyone? But Iron Man was the coolest to me. I think one of the reasons

I liked Iron Man was that in reality (if a comic book can be considered reality) he was just a regular guy. Tony Stark was just like you and me. He didn't come from another planet, he wasn't a mutant, and he hadn't been bitten by a radioactive spider. He was just a guy who was sick of the junk in the world around him, so he invented this really cool suit of iron with all kinds of gadgets on it, and bingo! He's a super-hero. I could do that, right? I could grow up and one day invent a suit and save the world. But when we do grow up, our fictitious heroes tend to be replaced by real people. Some of us look up to a big brother or a dad. Others idolize a teacher, pastor, or even a politician. Heroes can be found everywhere. We all need a hero. We need someone who appears greater than us, but fights the same battles we fight…and wins.

As a teenager, God called me into the ministry when I was 14. I knew from the summer of 1984 that I was going to spend my life serving God full time. I began to look for new heroes. One of my early heroes during this phase of my life was Dr. James W. Bryant, my pastor. I loved Dr. Jim. He was a great preacher and teacher. I soaked up his sermons each week, taking notes, and spending time during the week double-checking everything he said on Sundays.

My first opportunity to preach came the summer of my 17th year. Our church was going on a mission trip to help another church in Bloomington, Indiana. Man, I was excited and nervous. I had no clue how to even write a sermon, much less preach one. I will never forget Dr. Jim inviting me into his private study one afternoon and giving me a primer on how to prepare a sermon. Not only was it just cool to be in the "holy of holies," Dr. Jim's study, but I was honored that he would take his time and spend it on me. He was my hero.

I began to find other heroes of the faith as I moved through my teenage years. When I was 17, my family relocated to Salt Lake City, Utah and I landed my first ministry position.

It didn't matter that I was just an intern in my local church, I was actually drawing a paycheck. This just happened to be about the time that scandal hit the televangelistic world. Jim Bakker was embroiled in accusations of the rape of Jessica Hahn and he faced mounting pressure from allegations that he was defrauding people by selling time shares to his Heritage USA theme park. Bakker was later sentenced to 18 years in prison for his part in the fraud, and he served five of those years behind bars.

Then there was Jimmy Swaggart. Swaggart was extremely public in calling out the sin of Jim Bakker, going as far as to appear on Larry King Live and calling Bakker a cancer to the church. Then sin detonated in Swaggart's life when it became public he was engaging in activity with a prostitute, all caught on camera by a private investigator. Who can ever forget Jimmy's tearful and public confession, live on television?

To a young man headed into the ministry, the fall of these "heroes" was disillusioning. The week after the Swaggart confession I went to the local Smith's grocery store to cash my paycheck from the church. I will always remember the conversation I had with the customer service employee. She looked at the check from my church, asked to see my ID and said, "Oh, I guess we can trust a church...but you never really know anymore these days, huh?" Nuclear fallout.

God's Hall of (Sh)-(F)-ame

The truth is that heroes fall. That is because heroes are human and all humans are infected with the sin virus. The Bible is clear, "All have sinned and fall short of the glory of God" (Romans 3:23). All means all...even you, even me, even heroes.

If someone were to ask me, "Hey, Jeff, does God have a Hall of Fame?" I'd say, yes! The book of Hebrews contains a section that I call God's Hall of Fame. It is a list of the greatest of the greats from the Old Testament. Men and women who laid it all on the line.

If you want to see the greatest of the greats in professional football, you'd make a pilgrimage to Canton, Ohio, to the *Pro Football Hall of Fame*, pay $18, and spend a day reliving the greatest moments with the greatest personalities the game has ever seen. To relive the greatest moments in the Old Testament with the greatest personalities of the Bible, you would make a pilgrimage to Hebrews 11.

In Hebrews 11, you will see many familiar faces as you stroll the walkways of this Hall of Fame. You'll find yourself stopping at the exhibit for Noah. Who could forget Noah and the flood? What a man of the faith. When everyone was laughing and making fun of him for building a boat in the middle of the desert, Noah remained faithful. He pushed through. When the rain came and the water rose, Noah remained dry and his critics were all washed up.

You see people like Abraham. *"Father Abraham, had many sons...."* You remember the song. Yeh, that Abraham. Chosen by God. The father of a nation - God's people, from whom the savior of the world would one day come.

Then there's Isaac. Son of Abraham. Talk about a lot to live up to. But Isaac was one of the greats in his own right. He was a man of the future. A visioneer. He saw with clarity God's plan and placed great blessing on each of his two sons.

That's when we pass the exhibit for Jacob. Jacob was a man who understood worship. He went round for round with God. His specialty was wrestling. Jacob, the plaque says, was a worshipper even on his death bed.

There are other greats on display as well. There is Moses. The man who took on Pharaoh, the mightiest king in the world. He stood toe-to-toe and sent plague after plague until

Pharaoh had had enough. Moses, the parter of waters. A hero among heroes.

There are certain people you just have to see when you visit the Hall of Fame. David is one of those people. The greatest king in Israel's history. The warrior poet. A man's man. David the Beautiful, the writer of many psalms. David the Mighty, they slayer of lions and giants. Just one word says it all. David.

Oh, and don't forget the wing devoted to women. Oh, no, this is not just a man's club. Two prominent women can be found on display in the Hall. Every great man has a greater woman standing with him. For Abraham, it was Sarah. A woman of faith who believed in the promise of a son...at the age of 90. Don't miss Rahab. Some women tend to have a keen sense of whose side they need to be on. Rahab recognized God when she saw Him. Even living in the midst of a corrupt and godless city, she sided with God. She understood that if God is for us, who can be against us? She laid it all on the line when God's spies came on a reconnaissance mission. She provided "comfort and aid to the enemy." When the walls fell, Rahab stood.

There are so many others that you probably cannot see them all in one day. You'll have to come back another time. People like Gideon, Samson, Barak and Jephthah. You'll want to take your time and see them all. The greatest of God's greats. His Hall of Fame.

But God's Hall of Fame doesn't tell the whole story about these great heroes of the faith. You see, each of them, in their own way, was marked by the nuclear fallout of sin. As I stated earlier, you can't fight your genes. Now I will admit that growing up in church, I also grew up hearing all the wonderful stories about these and other great people in the Bible. As a child they became, in a very real sense, heroes. The heroes of the Bible. Because of the way the stories were always told, these people almost became superhuman in my imagination. That is good from the standpoint that we all need heroes, people to look up to. But it can be bad when these people become so BIG and great, that the average person can never live up to the model. I can never be Superman. I can't fly, see through walls, leap tall buildings in a single bound. You get the idea. The hero is out of reach. He's not real.

That's the way the people in the Bible became to me as I grew up. They were superhuman. I could never be like Moses. I hate locusts. No way I'm gonna call for thousands of them. Noah? No way. David? Not a shot. They weren't real to me.

Here's the deal: If all you read about these people is Hebrews 11, then you haven't seen the whole person. The Hall of Fame is only a picture of someone's career. Stop by the Roger Staubach exhibit at the *Pro Football Hall of Fame*, and you'll see highlights of his career. To see the full story, to really know the man, you'd have to go back and watch whole game films from his college career at Navy. Then you'd know why he won the Heisman Trophy. You'd need to watch whole seasons of his professional career with the Cowboys to understand why he was MVP of Super Bowl VI and considered one of the greatest quarterbacks of all time.

But in watching those game films you'd also discover that Roger Staubach was not perfect. You'd see his moments of shame along with his moments of fame. You see all the interceptions, all the fumbles, the missed snaps, and even games that were lost by bad decision-making. You'd see it all. The rest of the story. The whole story.

If you really want to know what the greatest of the greats in God's Hall of Fame were truly like, you need to go back and read the stories yourself; watch the game film. As Paul Harvey says, you need to hear, "The rest of the story…"

Noah

We all know the story of Noah and the flood. God looked down upon the earth and was angered and broken over the wickedness of mankind. Yet God saw something different in Noah. He was the only man found worthy by God to be spared. He was a hero. But then there was this very ugly scene once they get off the ark.

After a hard day's work, Noah went on a drinking binge and passed out drunk and naked in his tent. What followed is the source of some controversy, but one of Noah's sons, Ham, took advantage of the situation, leading to him ultimately being cursed.

Here we have Noah, the great hero, drunk and naked. Have you ever been drunk and naked? If so, you are in good company. My point? Noah was not perfect. He was a sinner too.

Abraham

What about Abraham? He was far from perfect as well. Abraham was really into himself. The Bible records a time that Abraham and Sarah were sojourning in Egypt. Now, Sarah must have really been a knockout because Abraham was afraid that when the Egyptians saw how beautiful she was, that they would kill him and take her. Abraham's solution? Lie. He instructed his wife to tell everyone that she was, in fact, his sister. Can you believe that? Abraham was so concerned about saving his own skin, that he was willing to run from his role as husband. As the story played out, Sarah caught the eye of Pharaoh himself and was taken into his harem. Abraham said nothing. Everything ended up working out okay because once Pharaoh found out the truth, he scolded Abraham, gave Sarah back, and sent them on their way. Lesson learned. Oh, but not quite.

The story actually repeated itself a second time. That's right. The same thing happened again. This time it was the region known as Gerar and the king was a man named Abimelech.

"Hey, Abe, whose that good lookin' girl you're with?"

"Uh… my sister."

"Cool, I think I'll marry her."

"Yeh…cool."

Once again, the truth came out and the couple was sent packing. Have you ever lied about your spouse and claimed they were your sibling? Sounds like a Jerry Springer episode, huh? But it's not. It happened to one of God's heroes. For all the great things he was, Abraham was also a sinner.

And the list goes on…

I could go on but I don't think I need to. I think you get the point. Each of God's heroes were, in their own way, flawed. They were sinners. Jacob was a liar and a thief of sorts. Moses was a murderer. David was a liar, murderer and adulterer. Rahab was a prostitute. The list goes on and on. And so does the sin.

Here is the most important thing I want you to see about these perfectly flawed people: Their sin did not define them. It was not the last word about who they were. The last word is found in Hebrews 11. When you walk through God's Hall of Fame, you don't see a Hall of Shame and sin. In fact, there is no mention of their sin at all. The rest of the story for these heroes is that yes, they were all sinners, but they were also created in the Image of God. That image may have been disfigured by the nuclear fallout of sin, but God refused to leave them that way. Somewhere along the way there was a recovery. The image was restored.

Your Sin...and Mine

Why is this important? Because it gives me *hope*. I have never murdered anyone or prostituted myself. I will admit to having told a few lies. I am all too aware of my own sin, although I am not willing to admit to the specifics in these pages. But I *will* confess that I sin. That makes me a sinner. So there, I've said it. I am a sinner. And as I said at the beginning of this chapter, so are you.

All of us may have different sins that dog us, but we are all sinners just the same. Let me go one step further and say that no matter what your sin, its root is really all about *you*. The sin of *self*. Go back and look at the Hall of Fame. Each sin committed by our heroes had its root in self. Just like in the Garden. Just like Adam. Ultimately, my sin is about me. And your sin is about you.

That is why it is important to understand that the last word on our heroes was not their sin. The last word was about who they were as the Image of God. I need to see David as a sinner because that makes him real. Knowing that Moses murdered a man and yet was used by God to confound Pharaoh and part the Red Sea not only makes him real, but makes me think that maybe God can use me too. It gives me hope.

All of this teaches me something about God as well. Let me finish this chapter by going back to the Garden of Eden. Remember the rule? Remember the consequence for breaking the rule? God said that on the very day the rule was broken, Adam and Eve would die. I explained that I believe that God is talking about a real physical death. I believe this is what Adam believed as well. So why didn't they die? I think the answer lies in the nature of God and it carries with it a tremendous message of hope for you and for me.

I believe that what we see by Adam and Eve not falling over dead the moment they ate the fruit is an important attribute of God: mercy. Oh, yes, God could have killed them. That was the consequence. The wages of sin is death. But He didn't kill them. Instead, God chose to extend mercy.

Did He have to? No.

Does He always? No.

But He did then and I believe He does today. Part of God's nature is that He is a merciful God. And you and I are created in the image of that God.

Chapter 2 – Lost

One of my favorite places on earth is Colorado. I love the sense of renewal that comes from being in the mountains. Each spring Julie and I go away for a week together. No kids. No calendar. No pressure. Just us. Our destination? Lost Valley Ranch smack in the middle of the Pike National Forest in Colorado. We load up the minivan with everything we'll need to enjoy ourselves for seven days away from it all. Julie takes her scrapbooks and I take a couple of good novels and my Wranglers. We leave early on a Saturday morning heading West on I-40. Kansas is the longest stretch, but it's not so bad as Julie and I just talk. After about 10 hours on the road, we can just start to see the outline of the Rocky Mountains. One thing I love about the mountains is that over the course of a year my life goes though all sorts of peaks and valleys, lots of change; but no matter how much life changes, the mountains are always there, like an anchor. I feel rooted and secure when I see those mountains. I am instantly reminded that no matter how crazy life may swirl around me, it doesn't affect the mountains. Here, it is safe. The mountains remind me that God and His creation are still intact.

I go to the mountains because I need to get away and replant myself. I need to connect with God in a way that I cannot connect with Him back home. I need to connect with my wife in a way that is impossible in the flow of the other 358 days of the year. Lost Valley Ranch is the perfect place to do this. Founded as a real working cattle ranch, the ranch has been owned by the Foster family for the last four decades. Bob and Karen Foster open their ranch to guests who are looking to get away from phones, television, and cell service. You won't find any of that there. You can spend your days horseback riding, fishing, hiking, sleeping, eating, or any combination of the above. The scenery is stunning and no matter where you go in the valley you will find God.

Julie and I love to hike when we go to Lost Valley. It is hands-down our favorite thing to do together. There are numerous peaks around the valley. If you want the signature hike of the ranch, take half a day and tackle Sheep Rock. If you want a brisk morning wakeup, head for Helen's Rock and get there around 6:15, just in time to see the sun crack the sky over Pike's Peak. Julie and I have been traveling to Lost Valley for the last six years and we have yet to climb them all. Several years ago, we set out for a new peak we had never been to — Southern Comfort. Located at the far end of the valley, it is a good 60 to 90 minute hike. We were told that it has one of the best views of the Pike's Peak side of the valley. A "can't miss" experience.

So after breakfast one morning, Julie and I donned our hikers, loaded our backpack with water, checked the camera for fresh batteries, and headed out. The first third of the hike was no big deal, just a walk out of the ranch area of the valley. The trailhead was easy to locate and we were off and away before we knew it. But after about 20 minutes, we hit a fork in the trail. We were operating off of a pretty crude trail map that doubled as a breakfast placemat in the lodge! As best we could tell, we needed to go right instead of straight. It was the wrong choice. After another 20 minutes or so, it became clear to me that we were not on the path that would take us to Southern Comfort. In fact, we had no idea where we were for sure...we were lost.

There is nothing worse than getting lost on a hike. You spend time selecting a destination. You pack the right equipment. Adrenaline is pumping and your spirits are high. But it is the anticipation of reaching the summit that is the killer. After all the "hype," reality starts to set in that you aren't going to make it. Then determination sets in: "Oh, yes we are! We *will* to find another way." That usually ends in getting yourself even more lost. That's the point Julie and I came to that day. We were frustrated and mad BUT we were going to make it to Southern Comfort one way or another. The trail we were on actually led us to a lower peak called Camera Rock. It was cool, but not where we wanted to go. We began to bushwhack our own trail. We were determined. We scrambled over rocks and hills, down into lower areas and back up rocks again. We saw a peak in the distance that had to be Southern Comfort. We scratched and clawed our way to the top, only to discover that there was another, higher peak just ahead on the ridge. Ahhhhh....we wanted to scream. So what rock *were* we standing on? I had no idea.... we were lost. Now we were really mad. We had come too far to turn back, so we pressed on to the next peak that just had to be the all-coveted Southern Comfort.

After more scrambling and bringing ourselves to the point of sheer exhaustion, we made it...but not to Southern Comfort. We were standing on what we would later discover was Angel Rock. A very impressive lookout, but not where we had wanted to go. But...we could finally see our destination. Southern Comfort was staring at us just head as the next and final peak on the ridge. It was also obvious that we could not get there from Angel Rock. We were forced to face reality, that Southern Comfort would have to wait another day. Angel Rock did give us our bearings, however, and so we were no longer lost. We found the trail back to the ranch and returned feeling defeated.

Getting lost does that to you. It is a mark of defeat. You are going somewhere and all of a sudden, the destination is in jeopardy. Sometimes you recover and make it, and sometimes you don't. In the midst of floundering, feelings of anger (how could this happen?), doubt (I must be an idiot), panic (I'll never get out of here), blame (this has to be someone's fault), abound. Being lost is a bad thing. Just like sin, being lost is a part of the human condition. In fact, being lost is part of the nuclear fallout of sin.

Midnight in the Garden of Good and Evil

Sin and evil entered the Garden when Adam chose self over God and his wife. Because of this, they could not stay. Evil had come to the Garden. God put it like this,

"Behold, the man has become like one of us in knowing good and evil." [1]

Now, there was another tree in the Garden: the Tree of Life. If you eat the fruit from this tree, you will live forever. It is a tree that sustains eternal life. But evil must have an end, sin must be punished. Because of His nature, God cannot allow evil to go on forever and sin to go unpunished. Adam and Eve had to suffer the consequences for their sin: Be removed from the Garden and from their home, never to return.

We are told that God *drove* Adam and Eve out of the Garden. This is an interesting word used to describe the expulsion of Adam and Eve. It is the Hebrew word *gaw-rash*. It means to cast out or thrust out. It is a word that represents a complete cutting off. *Gaw-rash* can also mean *divorce*. I think that is very interesting. What happened to Adam and

Eve was a severing of their relationship with God, as we have already seen. The term *divorce* indicates the level of intimacy with God that has been *lost*. The marriage is over. Ended. There is grieving for what once was, what was hoped for, and for what has now been lost; just like in a marriage between a man and a woman when it ends in divorce. Most divorced people will tell you that their divorce led to feelings of disorientation in terms of their life. Where am I going? What will tomorrow be like? Can I ever pull it back together? How can I go on? Can I ever love again? Can I ever be loved again? This is all the language of being lost.

The Lost Kingdom

Adam and Eve found themselves lost in a big world. Home base, the Garden, was no longer accessible to them. The Tree of Life was out of reach and mortality would take its toll. They began to live their lives the only way they could live them. Forging some form of society in an untamed frontier world. They had children and their children began to have children and the world began to be populated.

Sin also populated the new world as Adam's original sin nature was passed on to everyone of his seed. One of Adam's descendants was Nimrod. We are told that Nimrod was the first on the earth to be a mighty man. Nimrod was the first politician, a man of the people. He was charismatic and strong. He had a keen mind and knew the art of persuasion. People gravitated to Nimrod as a leader. He was a mighty hunter, a slayer of great beasts. While everyone else was eating tomato soup, Nimrod was eating steak.

The Bible records that Nimrod's kingdom began at Babel and encompassed the additional territories of Erech, Accad, and Calneh. All of these were located on the plain of Shinar. You remember the kingdom of Babel, don't you? Nimrod began his rule of earth's first empire at Babel. The word *babel* means confusion. Don't miss this important detail that the world's first kingdom was born out of confusion. Babel was the Lost Kingdom led by Nimrod the Mighty.

Nimrod pulled people together from all over the region. He convinced them that they had all they needed among themselves. *"We don't need God, we have each other... us!"* To prove it, a construction project was begun; it was a project using the latest in architectural technology. Man had discovered the process of firing mud and stone to form bricks. They had mastered the process of using bitumen for mortar. This was cutting-edge stuff. Who needs a Garden built by God when we can build our own refuge with our own hands? More than that, a godless people would build a tower of brick and mortar to heaven. They would build a throne for themselves higher than the throne of God. They would establish themselves in the highest of the clouds. They would be where God was and yea, higher than God.

Sound familiar?

The sin of self...again.

God would have none of it. What did He do? Knock down their tower of blocks with His mighty hand? No. God went one better. He created different languages. It almost sounds anti-climactic. Wouldn't an apocalyptic, doomsday display of God's power have been more appropriate and fitting? Not really. What God wanted to do was simply remind them of their place in this world. Like it or not they were *lost*. There was nothing that neither they nor Nimrod could do about it.

Imagine you are in the scene that day. You're working on a wall. Everyone is excited. Oh, sure, it's not glamorous work, but you are participating in the most fantastic construction project in the history of man. As you proudly lay brick upon brick, you hope that any minute Nimrod will come around and compliment your work. There is just something about his presence that provides daily reassurance that you're doing what you were called to do in life. As you are chatting with your neighbor about the need for more mortar, you notice him looking at you in a funny way. What's *his* problem? Why is he just staring at you? Then you notice others staring. You ask them what is wrong. They begin to talk to one another, and not only can you not understand what they are saying, but it is clear that they cannot even understand each other. In fact, as you look around at the 15 people working in your section, panic sets in as no one can understand anything anyone is saying. In an instant, life has changed forever. A distinct feeling of lostness sets in.

The chaos of that day is difficult to imagine. In my first year of college, I visited a church one Sunday morning. There were a lot of new college students that Sunday since it was the beginning of a new semester, so we had an ice-breaker. You know, those really stupid activities that no one wants to do, but everyone does anyway because you *have* to go along. The ice-breaker of the day was a classic. It was the one where everyone is given a slip of paper with the name of an animal on it. You are supposed to look at the name on your paper and not show anyone else. When they say "Go," you're supposed to make the sound of that animal and walk around the room until you find the other people who have the same animal sound as you. Sounds like fun, huh? Yeh, that's what I thought too.

I found myself walking around the room yelping like an elephant, feeling like a complete fool, looking for other people yelping like elephants. It was a low point in my life. As you can imagine, it was chaos. But in a weird way it was sort of fun, and when it was over we all went back to pretending to be people again. But what if it never ended? What if the chaos was permanent? That was Babel. No amount of charisma or politicking by Nimrod could change a thing. Construction came to a screeching halt and the people scattered, frantically looking for someone, anyone, with whom they could communicate. All this was God's reminder to a lost world that they really were *lost*.

Ways We Are Lost

There is more than one way to be lost. The condition of lostness reveals itself in life at various times and in various ways. If you live life long enough you will experience each of these forms of lostness to varying degrees. The Image of God has been disfigured and this is what it looks like. I might point out that all the following ways in which we are lost will be completely abolished in heaven.

Geographically Lost

I have resisted buying a GPS. Everybody that I know who owns one swears by it. I just haven't made the jump yet. I'm a map man. My dad was an over-the-road truck driver for over 40 years and he was a Rand McNally Road Atlas man. That's what I use, too. Like father like son. I have one in my truck and one in our van. When my children leave the home, I will present them each with their own Rand McNally Road Atlas. I don't ever want them to get lost.

That's the point of a road atlas. To keep you from getting lost. You know where you are and where you are going. You can see all the various ways to get to where you want to go. That's the point of a GPS as well. It is just more of Man's technology designed to keep us from getting lost as we travel. But even with an atlas I have gotten lost before, especially if I travel rural roads to remote places. You can get lost with a GPS too. What if the batteries go out? All technology has limits.

For many years I served on the staff of Shiloh Christian School in Springdale, Arkansas. A highlight of my job was football season. I used to love Friday nights, watching the

Shiloh Saints play 3A football all over the state of Arkansas. The 3A classification had me traveling to some out-of-the way places. I almost always needed directions to find the local football stadium in places like Pea Ridge, Green Forest, and Cedarville. Every football season, at some point I would get lost. There is a joke that men don't like to ask for directions. That's especially true on a Friday night when you roll into a town with only one stoplight, wearing the colors of the opposing football team! That is definitely a feeling of being lost.

Geographical lostness is a very real thing. The Garden of Eden was home to Man. It was the location of the Tree of Life. It was a physical location that was no longer accessible to the children of Adam. Today, we have no idea where the Garden of Eden was. It was probably located some place in present day Iraq, but no one knows for sure. God will not allow us near it because of the Tree of Life. We must suffer the consequences of sin. We are lost whether we like it or not. We are lost whether we realize it or not.

Life Direction: Which Way Should I Go?

I had a life crisis when I turned 30. I'm talking about the whole dynamic of saying goodbye to my 20s and actually turning 30 years old. I know this may all sound silly, but I think everybody goes through this same thing at some point. For some it is 40, for some it is 50 or 60. For me it was 30. You can ask my wife and she will tell you how weird I became as I approached my 30th birthday.

I cannot speak for everyone else, but for me it was a coming together of several factors that created a sense of panic in me when I hit 30. First, I became very aware that at 30, I was well on my way, in terms of age, toward my peak earning years. The experts say those peak earning years come between the ages of 40-45. When I turned 30 it hit me like a load of bricks that my 20s had flown by. It seemed like only the blink of an eye since I had graduated from college, and now I was turning 30? It made me realize that 40 would come just as quickly if not quicker, so I found myself weighing my place in this world.

At the age of 30, I was making less than what I thought I should be making, I had almost no savings account, and had virtually no plan in place for my retirement as my employer offered nothing. I remember just having that sense that no matter how much I enjoyed what I was doing, it wasn't getting me anywhere (at least where I thought it should get me). I had a sense I was not doing all I could to take care of my family. I had two kids at the time and I had aspirations of being able to send them to college one day. I basically didn't know where I was going in life. I was depressed and I was lost.

As I said, I think we all find ourselves at those points in life where we just don't know where we are going. We aren't satisfied with the path we are on and we have a strong sense that we were meant for something more, that we are capable of something more. I call it the *"I don't know what I want to be when I grow up"* syndrome.

I have a very good friend named Dave. Dave is just a few years older than me and by all accounts he has made it in life. He has a beautiful wife and wonderful family. He owns his own business and is just knocking it out of the park financially. He has a great home, cars, all the toys he wants. God has blessed him tremendously. But there is something missing in Dave's life. He recently confided in me that all the "stuff" he has accumulated means nothing to him. What he really wants to do is make a difference. He wants to do something bigger than himself. He wants to leave something behind for others. He is just not quite sure where to go with it all. In a way, he is lost and is just not sure which direction to take.

Both of our stories highlight what is a common condition for all of us at some point in life. The point of being lost. Not knowing what direction to go in life. Should I change jobs? Should I move? Does my wife need to work? Does she need to stay home? Should we start that business? What can I do with the overflow? All these questions highlight the human condition. We are lost.

Family (dis)Connections

Several years ago our family took the great American vacation to California. All 1600 miles in a minivan. It was actually great, the best vacation our family has ever taken. We did Disneyland, Hollywood, the whole southern California experience. One particular day we decided to take the kids to Pismo Beach. It was our first family trip to a real beach of any kind.

I will tell you that one of the most frightening moments of my life occurred that day on the sands of the Pacific. Julie and I were about 40 yards inland and had set up a base of sorts with all our blankets, towels, food, etc. Our two oldest children, Madison and Garrett, had gone to play in the ocean and we had instructed them to be sure to stay with the people they knew, to stay in front of us, and to not go too far out into the water. I would occasionally run out there to mess with them and have some fun.

At one point, I had been up by our "base" for quite a while playing with our youngest son Grayson, and just chatting with other people around us. I looked up to spot the two older kids and I couldn't see Garrett. At first it was not a big deal because there were a lot of people in and out of the water. The more I looked, the more worried I became. I couldn't find him. I am not one to sound a premature alarm, so I just calmly got up and made my way to the shore line, certain that I'd see Garrett at any moment. As I reached the water, still no luck. A sense of dread began to set in. I yelled back at Julie to see if she had seen Garrett. She instantly knew something was wrong.

At that point, things became pretty fuzzy. I will admit that sheer panic began to set in. I began to yell for Garrett, but to no avail. I will never forget the sensation that settled over me at that moment. Surrounded by people playing and laughing, I felt totally alone, as if disaster had struck and no one noticed. My sole thought was that Garrett had been grabbed by an undertow and pulled out too deep. All I could think of was: That is my son, my first born, "out there" somewhere, and I cannot find him. I didn't even know where to begin to find him. I also had the sensation that it was already too late.

As people started joining us in our search, I found myself frantically wading out chest deep into the ocean, only to lose my whole sense of orientation. I was overwhelmed by the sheer feeling of love that I have for my son and the thought that I would never hold him again; that our journey of 10 years together had come to a cruel and immediate end. Not only was my son lost, but I felt lost without him. It brings tears to my eyes even now to re-live the events of that day in writing. I will never forget that moment. Ever.

All of a sudden, Garrett came walking up the shoreline, oblivious to the frantic search by his parents and the people around him. The sense of relief and rebirth that came over me was overwhelming. What had happened? Very simply, the right to left flow of the ocean had slowly nudged Garrett far down the shore without him even realizing it. It wasn't a big deal really, something that I am sure happens all the time. But to newbies to beach life such as the Crawfords, it was all new and unexpected to us.

What I learned that day was how critical family connections are to our lostness in this world. Death is real. Mortality comes with our sin. When the death of a family member or close friend occurs, we are reminded of how lost we really are on this earth. If I ever lost one of my children, I would be lost. If I ever lost Julie, my wife, I would be profoundly lost. It is not good that a man should be alone.

Yesterday I traveled to Tulsa, Oklahoma to attend the funeral of a dear aunt of mine, Aunt Betty. My Aunt Betty was a remarkable woman. My memories of her from my childhood are too numerous to recount here. I truly loved her, and her funeral was an amazing tribute to a life lived for God and for her family. I was struck by how alone and lost my Uncle Bob looked without her. My Uncle Bob is a strong, godly man and pillar of his church, the First Baptist Church of Tulsa. But he had just lost his bride of 52 years and now, in a very real way, he was lost. I grieved with and for him. It reminded me of how lost we all really are. Our family connections take the edge off of that sense of lost-ness, then death shocks us back into reality. We are lost.

Spiritually Lost

This is the most critical and dangerous form of lostness and it is common to all people. Because of our DNA of sin, we are all born in a condition of being spiritually lost. This is a condition that we all live with 24/7 from the moment of conception.

At our core, we are much more than just physical beings. This is important to understand. Atheists proclaim that man is nothing more than meat, flesh and bones, and that life is nothing more than what we live on this earth. When we die, it is ashes-to-ashes and dust-to-dust. We cease to exist. People who do not believe in God are driven to think this way because they deny anything supernatural and embrace only nature. Nature dictates the doctrine of evolution, which says that all of this, the world and everything in it, including you and me, is just an accident. They are wrong. They are wrong largely because they, too, are lost.

The truth is that there is indeed a supernatural world that exists alongside the natural world. When I teach and preach on these things, I go as far as to assert that the supernatural world is actually *more* real than the natural world. I majored in philosophy in college, so I love to engage in these kinds of mind exercises. Philosophers call all of this metaphysics, or the study of what is real.

You don't have to be a Christian to believe in the supernatural. Actually, most of the population of the earth believes firmly in the supernatural. The atheist or naturalist is, in reality, in the minority. But not all supernaturalists think the same way about the supernatural. That is because they are lost, too. You can even think straight about the supernatural world and still be lost. On a spiritual or supernatural level, the starting point for all of us is the condition of being lost.

The supernatural world is around us and it is very real. Using the Bible as our text, we see God before we see nature. "In the beginning God...." Then we see God breathing the life or *spirit* into the first man. Spirit comes first. At the end of the Bible, in the book of Revelation, we see God concluding His work with this earth by destroying it. The natural ceases to exist, but we do not. That is because we are, at our core, spiritual. God then moves to re-create a new earth. All that is physical and natural flows from God, the ultimate supernatural being. Remember, *we* are made in the Image of God. The implications of all this will be explored much more deeply in chapter 10.

We are, in our essence of being, spiritual. As I said, we are all spiritually lost. This is a huge problem. Having explored the condition of lostness in this chapter, we know that to be found or located is much better than being lost. I think that most people are aware on some level that they are spiritually lost, and thus they are on a search. When people are lost, they search. But what are they searching for? The answers.

At the beginning of this book, I said that all people are looking for the answers to four questions: Where did I come from? Who am I? What is wrong with me? How do I fix it? Listen, these are all spiritual questions! The questions in and of themselves indicate our spiritual nature in spite of what the naturalist says.

Let's look just very quickly at how the naturalist or the atheist would answer these questions. Where did I come from? Accidental evolution, nothing else. Who am I? Flesh and bone, nothing more. What is wrong with me? Nothing, you are perfectly fine. If you think something is wrong with you, that is just religion making you feel guilty. And so there is no need for the final question.

But here is the problem with the atheist's answers to these questions: They just don't wash with people! Especially the answer to the question about what is wrong with me. I am telling you from years of experience, that everybody, including the atheist (if they would admit it), recognizes that something is just plain wrong, with themselves and with the world. No one in their right mind can look at this world and declare that it is perfect. Planes fly into buildings; children are kidnapped, raped and murdered; pornography is an out-of-control virus; and the two major political parties in this country can only point fingers at each other. Things are messed up, people know it, and people want to know why. I would even argue that the desire to want a solution to the "problem" is indication that something much more than animalistic, evolved thinking is going on in us. Something moral exists in us. Morals cannot be explained by evolution. They come from our spiritual nature and from God's image imprinted on us. We are spiritual beings.

So the third question, "What is wrong with me?" is at its core a spiritual question. What is wrong, my friend, is that you are lost. That is why you have this nagging sensation that all is not well with your life, that you are missing something. It's not a better job or more money. It's not a new boyfriend or going back to school that is going to give you the answer. Deep down you know it. Deep down you know you are lost. Once you realize that, you are ready for the next question. How do I fix it? We will talk about that later.

Lost and Not Knowing It

Some people get lost and don't know it. That is probably the worst condition to be in. The longer you drive in the wrong direction, before stopping to ask for directions, will just get you more lost. Yes, there are varying degrees of lostness.

Park rangers will tell you that when you are out hiking and you first realize that you are lost, STOP and just sit down. People who try to fix their own situation will just make matters worse. If you keep walking, you will get more lost. You make finding the path back much harder and much more complicated. You will most likely need to be rescued if you are truly lost, and the further you go, the wider the search area becomes and the harder it is and the longer it takes to rescue you.

But some people are stubborn. They just refuse, in spite of all the signs, to admit that they are lost. I think that goes back to the "sin of self" conversation from the last chapter. We are prideful people and we want to think we can do it on our own. It's not surprising that this is the case. It is really very easy to be lost and not know it. Oh, you might suspect it and have that feeling that something is not right, but to know for certain can be hard.

C.S. Lewis is perhaps my favorite author of all time. I am convinced that he is the greatest Christian mind of the last century. I read a lot of books and I can tell you that hands-down, C.S. Lewis is quoted by other authors more than anyone else I see. I will throw my own Lewis quote in at this point. Lewis commented in his masterpiece on apologetics, *Mere Christianity*, that "A man does not call a line crooked unless he has some idea of a straight line."[2] And he is right. I think that the reason many people are lost and just don't know it is because they have never known what it was like to *not* be lost, to be *found*. Since all they've ever known is crooked, they cannot even fathom what straight would be like. I hope the words of this chapter have served to give you but a vague glimpse of what straight is. Act 2 of this book will go much deeper, giving you a much clearer line to follow. So keep reading.

Chapter 3 – Hungry

Have you ever been hungry? I mean *really* hungry? Hunger is a relative term, isn't it? I just ate lunch about two hours ago because I was hungry. It had been about four-and-a-half hours since I had eaten breakfast. As I am writing this I can sense my stomach calling out for a snack. I will try to not give in (I seem to be more easily gaining weight these days) and instead wait until dinner around 6:30 this evening. I'll probably top off the day with a "small" bowl of ice cream around 8:30 pm. Then I'll just start all over tomorrow.

Isn't it funny how our whole day is organized around food? When we get hungry we eat. We actually plan the rhythm of our days around meal times. It's as if, in a very real sense, food controls our schedules.

As I said, hunger is a relative term. Most of us will experience hunger several times in the course of a day, but at the same time, most of us could skip a meal if we had to without going "hungry." So, let me ask again. Have you ever been *really* hungry? If I am honest with myself and with you I will admit that I have claimed to be starving at various times in my life. The truth is, I have never been starving. But I was really hungry one time in my life.

In 2001, I took part in a 10 day fast from all solid food. I allowed myself juice and broth, nothing else. It was one of the hardest things I have ever done. I used the opportunity of my fast to seek God's will for my life in a very particular and private area. That's the whole idea of a fast, empty yourself of food in order to be filled up with God. We'll talk more about this later.

The fast did other things for me as well. For the first time in my life, it hit me as to how controlled I really am by food. Think about it, we literally surround ourselves with food and with images of food. If you work in an office, I'll bet you have a work room with a refrigerator right now that is stuffed with food, some of it probably spoiled. You may even have your own refrigerator in your office, I do. When I was in college, it was a must to have your own personal refrigerator. It is not uncommon on any given week for people in our office to bring food to work to share with one another. Almost all of us have our own "stash" of food in a drawer or cabinet. I've got some Pay Days, peanut butter crackers, cereal bars, and beef jerky at my personal disposal right now.

Consider for a moment the advertising on television. As an experiment, sit down one evening and just keep a record of how many ads include food as their hook. Restaurants, beer, sodas, and individual ads highlighting specific food items. It's all over the place. There is even the Food Network on cable now. How many morning shows have a food segment? Emeril even had his own sitcom for a while until people figured out he could cook better than he could act. Pick up a magazine and just count the number of food ads. Food is everywhere, all around us, all the time. If someone from another planet were to visit, they might even think we worship food, and perhaps we do.

My fast also taught me how much I crave and fixate on food. Throughout my fast, I couldn't quit thinking about it. Everywhere I went, I saw the food that everyone else was eating that I couldn't eat. And the smells! Ah…those were the killers. I had the misfortune of taking a trip to Washington D.C. while I was on my fast. I say misfortune because everywhere I went in the nation's capital there was food. Shortly after landing, I took a train from Baltimore to Union Station and as soon as I left the platform, I was hit with wave after wave of wonderful smells. I stayed in a really nice hotel that had what smelled like a fantastic restaurant. I'll never know though. I will say that their broth was out of this world. Try ordering broth at an upscale restaurant sometime and watch how the waiter looks at you.

This is how God made us. He made us to hunger and to thirst for things, the most obvious of which is food and water. When the Image of God was marred and disfigured in Eden, our sense of hunger also became marred and disfigured. Oh, we still hunger and thirst for things, but our focus and priorities as we seek to satisfy those hungers is what has become twisted. Knowing this, God set out to make it *hard*.

Back in Genesis chapter 3, as part of God's punishment for Adam's sin of "me first," God declared,

> *"Because you have listened to the voice of your wife and have eaten of the tree of which I commanded you, 'You shall not eat of it,' cursed is the ground because of you; in pain you shall eat of it all the days of your life; thorns and thistles it shall bring forth for you; and you shall eat the plants of the field. By the sweat of your face you shall eat bread...."*

What God meant is that food will no longer come easy. Forget about the days of hanging out in the Garden where the fruit just falls into the palm of your hand and where the animals bring you all manner of gifts to eat. Now you have to work. But the ground will not always cooperate. There will be good seasons and bad seasons, good years and bad years. Sometimes the rain will fall and sometimes it won't. Sometimes it won't quit raining and you might lose the crop.

When I was in seminary, I had the privilege of pastoring the Valley View Baptist Church in Spanish Fort, Texas. Julie and I would make the two hour plus drive every weekend to preach and minister to the good people of this remote rural town in Texas. They were good people. I was city and they were country and I think sometimes I learned more than they did. During the fall one year it was time to bring in the wheat crop. Now here's the thing about wheat I never knew until I was a pastor in Spanish Fort, Texas: Wheat has a small window whereby it needs to be brought in. If you miss the window, the whole crop is lost. One other important detail involves rain. Wheat has to be dry when it is harvested. Rain and the harvest don't go together when it comes to wheat.

It was a wet fall during this particular year and there had not been a break in the weather during the critical window of time for harvesting the wheat. I sensed real tension among the people. One of the godliest men in our congregation was James Carpenter. He was a rugged farmer and a patriarch of our church. James was nervous and he told me one Sunday what everyone knew, that the window of opportunity was closing. The financial impact on the people of our church could be devastating. On this particular Sunday I could tell that even though people's bodies were in the pews, their minds were in the fields. As I got up to preach, I put aside my sermon for the day and said what was on everyone's mind. The rain had to stop. The sun needed to come out, and now.

I asked the people to join me in prayer to ask God to dry the land. I invited anyone who wanted to, to come to the front and kneel and pray. I closed my eyes and began to offer our petitions to God. As I prayed I heard the rustling of footsteps, more than I was expecting. I decided to take a peek. Opening my eyes, every single person had left their seat and was kneeling at the front of the church. Never had I seen such desperation. I was struck at how truly reliant we are on God to meet our needs. All the advancements in farm technology couldn't control the weather; only God could. So we found ourselves asking God to dry the wheat. You know what? He did. That very week, the rains subsided and the sun dried the wheat in just the time that was needed to make the harvest window.

This is what God is talking about in Genesis. God makes us to hunger, and then He makes us to work for it. Since we have made the conscious decision that we don't need God, we just need ourselves, God puts in place a system whereby we have to put up *and* shut up. We must work the ground for everything we have, and even then that won't always be enough. In fact, if you live life long enough, you will find yourself running out of self and running to God. That's just the way He wants it.

Tempting Foods

The first temptation involved food. Remember our story in the Garden of Eden? Eve is out taking a walk and it must be close to lunch. They say you should never go to the grocery store when you're hungry. You'll spend more. And you should never walk by the forbidden tree at lunchtime. Playing off of our natural hungers, the snake offers a snack. "Psst. Eve! Over here. Is that your stomach I hear growling? Check out this fruit. Doesn't it look good? I've tried one and it is out of this world! Look, there's a ripe one. I'll bet that if you put your hand under it, it will just fall into your palm. You won't even have to pick it. God would never blame you for not letting food go to waste."

Actually, the Bible says it like this,

"So when the woman saw that the tree was good for food, and that it was a delight to the eyes...."

The temptation of food was used to take Eve's eyes off of God and to put them on herself and her own desires.

Let's look at one other very interesting case. The book of Matthew records a time period in the life of Jesus when he too participated in a fast. It says of Jesus in verse two of chapter four that,

"after fasting forty days and forty nights, he was hungry."

You could probably call that an understatement. First, notice that Jesus as the God-man experienced hunger, just like us who were created in the Image of God. Notice, too, in verse three, how Satan tries to exploit Jesus at one of his weakest points.

"And the tempter came and said to him, "If you are the Son of God, command these stones to become loaves of bread."

Satan tries to take advantage of the hunger of Jesus. He tries to play the same card on Jesus that he played on Eve. "Hey Jesus, take your eyes off of God and put them on yourself. You have all that you need within yourself. You don't need God. You *are* God! Just turn these rocks into bread and dig in!" But unlike Eve, Jesus does not give in. He rebuffs Satan's attacks and, in the act of doing so, retains his own *image* as the Son of God.

The Culture of Gluttony

These two temptation stories teach us something very important. Hunger is a powerful force and food is a powerful aphrodisiac. Satan knows this and he tries to use this on a daily basis to keep our eyes off of God and on ourselves. His goal is to repeat the disaster of Eden in our lives.

God's intent is for us to hunger, and for us to work and sweat to yield what we need in life. It is also God's purpose for us to come to the end of ourselves in the process in order to rely on God as our ultimate provider. It is Satan's purpose to keep our eyes completely off of God and only on ourselves. It is his trickery at work seeking to convince us that we will never come to the end of ourselves, and that all our hungers can be met within our own efforts.

Go back and read the last paragraph again.

It is important as we move on.

This is what Babel, the Kingdom of Nimrod, was all about: Eyes on us and off of God. We don't need Him, we only need ourselves. God busted all that up and He busts up our own efforts today, but we have become very good at moving on without God. Technology and science have created in us a false sense of self-reliance like humanity has never seen. We can irrigate deserts, we can desalinate the oceans. We can create our own power and pump it into our homes via electrical lines. We can actually turn on a faucet in our home and have clean water. We can travel to Wal-Mart and find virtually anything we need or want. We can communicate around the world on wireless phones. A GPS can tell me exactly where I am in the world at all times so that I am never "lost." Science provides the explanation of all life, of which we are a part. As we have harmed the global climate with all our pollution, we have it within our power to change the climate for good. We don't need God, we are world-shapers all by ourselves.

We have shaped our world to the point of gluttony. Gluttony is the sin of excess. We have mastered gluttony in our culture. When we think of gluttony, we most quickly think of food. According to the Centers for Disease Control and Prevention, one out of three adults are what they would define as obese. What is scarier is that one out of six teenagers is obese, and one out of seven preschoolers is obese.[1] We are successfully transferring what our own government calls a disease on to the next generation. There is much discussion regarding poverty in America, and it is true that many, many people live below the poverty line, yet in the midst of our discussions on poverty, we see gluttony.

We have even turned gluttony of food into a way to make money (another form of gluttony). The weight loss industry rakes in over $50 billion dollars a year.[2] Isn't it interesting that we actually have an entire "industry" for weight loss? Why? Because we are gluttonous. We just can't get enough.

Gluttony can take on many forms. We Americans love our stuff. We just can't seem to surround ourselves with enough stuff. Even our stuff has generated a whole industry. Because we have so much stuff, we can't fit it in our homes, so we have the self-storage industry. Did you know that there are 32,000 self-storage businesses in America with a combined total of 1.3 billion square feet of storage? That's enough storage space for every citizen to have their own four-and-a-half square-foot plot. Amazing.

Rubbermaid is making money off of our stuff, too. They sell each year approximately 100 million storage containers for us to put our stuff in. And if we are overwhelmed with all our stuff, there is someone to help out: the Professional Organizer. For around $75 an hour, a PO will come into your home and help you organize your stuff.

The gluttony of stuff. If we need something, we can get it. If we can't afford it, we can put it on credit. There are, seemingly, no limits. All of this flows out of a self-reliant spirit whereby we as the community of mankind have discovered ways to "till the ground" to the point of excess. We have successfully eliminated God from the equation. What this self-reliance has done is actually further marred the Image of God in us.

Think of it this way: Food is God's gift to us. When we eat in a moderate, healthy fashion the foods that are good for us, our bodies respond in a healthy manner. God expects us to work for our food and to rely upon Him to provide the ingredients we can't provide: rain, sun, etc. What we have done is taken God's gift and perverted it into the excess we call gluttony. When a person is gluttonous on food, God's gift disfigures their body rather than blessing it as God intends. Obesity physically distorts the body, but there are all sorts of internal distortions that take place: heart disease, hyper-tension, anxiety and stress, depression, diabetes, and liver disease. These all flow out of taking God's gift of food and using it to excess.

Jesus said that it is harder for a rich man to get into heaven than for a camel to go through the eye of a needle. I think if you look at that passage, you will see that the "rich" man was a person who had more than he needed. There was a form of gluttony in his life. He had achieved his status without the help of God, so he thought. Because of his reliance on self, his thinking had become perverted to the point that he didn't need God. Oh, he wanted the one thing money could not buy, which was heaven, but he did not want to become reliant upon God for it.

That is the root of gluttony. It is a demonstration of our success in life without God, and our unwillingness to rely upon God. But here's the thing…*God made us to hunger.* Physical hunger and a hunger for creature comforts force us to be reliant on God. You see, there is another kind of hunger that God does not want us to miss: a hunger for Him. When we gluttonize ourselves, we are really trying to satisfy our inward-most hunger for God. But this is a false satisfaction. Food and stuff can't fill our "hunger void" for God. Eventually we will find ourselves at the same place that the rich young ruler found himself: Having all the stuff in the world, but still hungry for God *and* unable to get to God because we simply will not turn complete control over to God. Hunger is a good thing. It reminds me that I am not in control and that I am not God. I am the Image of God and that image is messed up and I need God to fix me.

Our Four Greatest Hungers

Jesus was once asked what he thought was the greatest commandment in God's Law. Matthew 22:37 records that Jesus shot back without hesitation,

"You shall love the Lord your God with all your heart and with all your soul and with all your mind. This is the great and first commandment."

What Jesus was actually doing here was demonstrating his command of the Torah, which is the Jewish word for Law. The Torah consists of the first five books of the Old Testament: Genesis, Exodus, Leviticus, Numbers and Deuteronomy.

Jesus was quoting from Deuteronomy 6:5 which states,

You shall love the LORD your God with all your heart and with all your soul and with all your might.

There are two things I want you to notice about this quote from Deuteronomy. First, this command to love God immediately follows the *Shema*. The *Shema* is recorded in verse 4 and it says,

Hear, O Israel: The LORD our God, the LORD is one.

The *Shema* is the central point in Jewish worship recited by Jews on a daily basis as part of their morning and evening prayers. It is the focal point of Jewish monotheism: a declaration that there *is* a God, there is only *one* God, and that one God is deeply connected to His people. It is a worldview statement. It answers the first of our four big questions that all people ask. Where did I come from? God. And it paves the foundation for answering the second question. Who am I? God's. More specifically, I am made in the Image of God.

What follows the *Shema* is the greatest commandment: to love this God with all of one's being. The word *love* is a hunger word. I love my wife Julie. I hunger for her. I hunger to love and to be loved. When I travel, when we are separated, the hunger pangs become intense. I long to hear her voice. I imagine the smell of her hair and the warmth of her touch. I hunger. It is the same, but much more so with God. Because of Eden, we are separated, the Image of God is deformed, we are not whole. We hunger for what only God can give us.

Second, notice that Jesus uses the word *mind* in the book of Matthew in place of the word *might* as we see it in the book of Deuteronomy. We have two other accounts of this question as it was posed to Jesus in the books of Mark and Luke. In both of these accounts, we see a blending of the two quotations above with the exhortation to love God with all of one's heart, soul, mind and strength.[3] Craig Blomberg explains that "both (accounts) refer to wholehearted devotion to God with every aspect of one's being, from whatever angle one chooses to consider it – emotionally, volitionally, or cognitively."[4]

From the aspect of hunger, we hunger for God with the totality of our being. Because the Image of God has been disfigured, we hunger for God in the depths of our being. These depths are expressed in four areas: heart, soul, mind, and strength.

Heart Hunger

The heart is the emotional seat of who we are as human beings. When someone is calloused, we use phrases like, "Have a heart, will you?" If someone is sad and distraught, we say that they have a "broken heart." During the course of any given day, my heart may ride the roller coaster of emotion. Emotions are powerful. Emotions drive us to action.

By our very nature, we want our hearts to be happy and full of joy. Anytime we are in a state of sadness and despair, we seek to fix our hearts. We hunger to be happy again. Most of the time we have it within ourselves to be happy once again.

It is said that time heals all wounds. That is partly true. Time does heal many wounds, or at least it creates a scar that enables us to function normally again, to be happy again. But sometimes we need help to heal our hearts. Friends and family can help, but sometimes we need professional help.

The whole psychotherapy profession exists to help restore people to emotional balance and health. To restore people's hearts. This can be accomplished through therapy and medication. You can talk to any good counselor and they will tell you that they are overwhelmed with clientele.

One of the pastors on our staff specializes in counseling people who are hurting. Having a licensed counselor on our staff has been eye-opening. Once word got out that we provide this service, we became inundated with clients from in and out of our church seeking help with their "heart" problems. The sheer popularity of counselors and therapists is evidence of the enormous amount of heart hunger that people are experiencing today.

Soul Hunger

The soul is very different from the heart and sometimes people get them confused. Whereas your heart is the seat of who you are emotionally, your soul is the seat of who you are spiritually. Another way to put it is that the soul is the seat of *Whose* you are spiritually. You see, the soul has the ability to be possessed or shared by another. The book of Mark, chapter 5, records the story of a man who was possessed by demonic spirits. His soul had been taken hostage.

Jesus was traveling one day through the area of the Garasenes and he landed in a certain village by boat. As soon as he stepped foot on shore, a man whose soul had been taken captive by demonic spirits ran and fell before him. The man was completely out of control. His family and friends had tried to subdue him even to the point of chaining him. Occupation of his soul had a physical consequence as well. Through super-human strength, he was amazingly able to break the chains, and he had held up in the tombs with those who were physically dead. He no longer bathed, or cut his hair, or took care of his bodily hygiene in any way. He even resorted to cutting and bruising himself. The townspeople thought he had lost his mind, but Jesus knew he had lost his soul.

The soul has no real physical dimensions. Jesus learned that this man's soul was occupied by a horde of evil spirits calling themselves Legion. A Roman legion contained 4,000 to 6000 men. Jesus exorcised the demonic mob from the man and he immediately became himself again. It is interesting to note that the demons begged to be sent to a herd of pigs rather than be disembodied completely. Jesus accommodated their request and the pigs ran themselves off a cliff to sure death. Does this mean animals have souls as well? I think so. But animals are much different than people. People are made in the Image of God and animals are not. What makes the soul of a man different from the soul of an animal, I believe, is the function of the heart. You see, animals don't have "hearts." They operate purely off of instinct. Oh, you can say they have feelings of happiness and sadness. That may be true, but animals don't possess moral inclinations. They can't think communally or globally. They don't have guilty consciences. Humans experience all of this because our souls work in concert with our hearts, minds and bodies.

Mind Hunger

The mind is the seat of the intellect. Human beings hunger for knowledge. We are inquisitive and we want to know more. We are fascinated by the unanswered question. Why do we read? To learn. Why do we teach? To pass on knowledge. Children are a great example of mind hunger. They always want to know how and why. My son Grayson is six. He is a question machine. Recently, he wanted to know *where* God is. Julie told him God was in heaven.

"Where's heaven?"
Great question. "Ummm...up there."
"Can I go visit?"
"No, it doesn't work that way."
"How does it work?"
"Well, heaven is where you go when you die."
"Am I going to die?"
"Yes, someday."
"Will I go to heaven?"
"Well, if Jesus lives in your heart."
"Where do I go if he doesn't?"
"Oh boy...well, there's another place called hell."
"Where's hell?"
"Down there."
"Can I go visit?"

And it goes on and on. There are days it seems like Grayson is suffering from mind starvation! All his questions keep us on our toes and force us to learn and to teach and to feed our minds as well as his.

Consider technology. Technology is the evidence of new knowledge put into practice. We are not satisfied with our world as it is and we want to change it. I remember the day my dad brought home our first microwave as a kid. What was this new technology? He said it would make my mom's life easier. The first thing we cooked in our new microwave was bacon. Until microwaves, you had to cook bacon in a pan on the stove. It took a long time, something like seven to ten minutes. Talk about the dark ages. But with the microwave, the world of bacon cooking was forever changed. In just 90 seconds we had a hot sizzling piece of bacon ready to be gobbled up. Wow! How cool. It was fast, easy, and there was no pan to wash afterward.

How did we get microwave ovens? Someone wasn't satisfied with cooking bacon on a stove. They wanted to learn how to do it better. The human mind went to work, and presto —microwave ovens. That is how it goes. Our minds aren't satisfied with the status quo; they are starved for something more, so they go to work, and learn, and produce.

The capacity of the mind is also astonishing. The journal of *Brain and Mind* has determined that one human brain has more storage capacity than all the computers ever created. The average computer can store 10,000,000,000,000 bytes of information. The human brain can store bytes (they say) to the tune of 10 followed by 8,432 noughts.[5] How they know this, I don't know. What is more perplexing is that we still don't really know *how* the brain does all that it does. It is a mass of flesh with nerves and neurons that somehow communicate. When you put all this together it means we are able to learn and remember, and that the capacity of our storage banks isn't even close to full. Obviously God made us to *know*.

Strength Hunger

The body is the seat of physical hunger. This goes far beyond just our stomachs, it encompasses everything we are or are not physically. Our bodies cry out to be healthy. When we are sick we see this sense of physical hunger on full display. I caught the flu this past winter, and man, it just leveled me. In the course of two days I went from feeling great to feeling like I had one foot in the grave. My throat was scratchy and sore. I had severe body aches and my head was killing me, classic flu symptoms. My body was starving to feel good again. The flu is like that, you don't appreciate how good you feel until it is all taken away.

There is the "frog in the kettle" syndrome. You know how it goes. Throw a frog in a pot of boiling water and he'll jump out. But put him in a pot of room temperature water and put the heat on low and he'll just stay in there until he boils along with the water. Our physical bodies are the same way. We get hit by the flu one day and we're like, "Man, get me some drugs. I need to feel better *now!*" But most of us live our lives in a pot of slowly boiling water. Our bodies are starving for health and we don't realize it.

My wife, Julie, took up running about five years ago. I had tried to run track in high school and hated it. Hate is really too nice a word. Every fiber of my being detested running, but I was very supportive of my wife. She'd roll out of bed before the sun was up and I'd give her my thumbs up as I rolled over and pulled the sheets over my head.

Then one year on our annual trek to the mountains of Colorado, Julie and I were on one of our hikes that we love so much. I noticed that she was outpacing me by a mile. I was huffing and puffing and doubled over and she wasn't even breaking a sweat. It kind of ticked me off to be truthful. I am the "man" after all. I came back from that trip and decided I probably needed to get into shape. So I went out and bought a pair of running shoes and declared to Julie that she now had a running partner.

I rolled out of bed one dark morning, and Julie and I hit the asphalt. Our goal was three miles. I hung pretty good for one mile. It was a killer. I was breathing so loud Julie thought I was going to wake up the neighbors. It was one of the worst mornings of my life. When we got back to the house, I collapsed on the living room floor and turned the ceiling fan on full blast. I was sweating profusely and thought my heart was going to explode out of my chest. That lasted a full 30 minutes. It all sounds funny now, but I determined that morning that I was seriously out of shape. The kettle was boiling and I was cooking. My body was crying out in hunger for physical health and I hadn't been listening.

Our bodies will do that. They will give us signs of the level of physical hunger they are experiencing, but we have to be listening.

The Hunger of a King

Throughout its history, the nation of Israel had good and bad kings. The greatest of the kings of Israel was David. There was none like him before or after. Ask a Jew today who the greatest king in Israel's history was and he'll say David. After David came his son Solomon. Solomon was good, but not as good as David. After Solomon, an up and down roller coaster of good and bad kings took off. When leadership suffers, the people suffer. This was the case for the nation of Israel as a whole. You can read the books of 1 and 2 Kings to see this. In the absence of good, strong, and godly leadership, the people became self-reliant and turned away from God.

One king came along, however, who was special. His name was Josiah. You can read his story in 2 Kings 22-23. He was an amazing man. He actually began to reign when he was eight years old, a child king. When Josiah was 26 years old, something extraordinary happened to him, he found a Bible. Things had gotten so bad in the nation of Israel that the ancient scrolls containing God's Word had actually been lost. Imagine a church with no Bibles. They're just gone, and on top of that, no one cares.

That's the situation in Israel when Josiah takes over. In the process of cleaning out the temple, the high priest finds a copy of the Torah. Knowing the heart of his king, he delivers the book to Josiah and for the first time in his life Josiah reads the Torah, God's Law. It has a profound impact on his life. We are told that this king is moved to the point of tearing his clothes. The hunger that had been consuming this young king is suddenly filled with God's Word.

Amazing things begin to happen after this. Josiah orders the destruction of all the pagan Baal temples. He rounds up the Baal priests and has them executed. He outlaws the wicked practice of child sacrifice to the god Molech that had become prevalent among God's own people. The nation of Israel was boiling to death and didn't know it, but their king did and he was on a mission to save the nation whether they liked it or not.

Out of the whole two chapter account of Josiah's kingship, one verse stands out,

"Before him there was no king like him, who turned to the Lord with all his heart and with all his soul and with all his might, according to all the Law of Moses, nor did any like him arise after him."[6]

Look at that verse closely. Three words jump out at me as I view this text: heart, soul, might. This is no accident. Josiah read the Torah, and built his life and reign around what Jesus would later declare is the greatest of all the commandments in the Law. Josiah recognized that everything about his being was crying out in hunger. That hunger was placed there by God and God was the only one who could fill him. As a king he *was* the rich young ruler, but unlike the rich young ruler that Jesus encountered, Josiah knew that nothing in *this* world would satisfy the hunger of his heart, soul, mind and strength.

Josiah fed the hunger of the nation of Israel by getting rid of any and all replacements to the worship of the one true and living God. Baal, Molech, mediums, necromancers, and all the rest were jettisoned from the culture. But Josiah did more. He didn't just remove, he added. He reinstituted the Jewish feasts that had not been celebrated by God's people since the time of the judges. These feasts were critical to Jewish worship because they were a tangible demonstration of God's love for His people and their reliance on Him for all their hunger needs. Notice this verse which describes Josiah's commanded return to the nation's religious roots,

> *And the king commanded all the people, "Keep the Passover to the Lord your God, as it is written in this Book of the Covenant." For no such Passover had been kept since the days of the judges who judged Israel, or during all the days of the kings of Israel or of the kings of Judah.*
>
> *But in the eighteenth year of King Josiah this Passover was kept to the Lord in Jerusalem.*[7]

Passover was more than just a holiday or a feast. In fact, Passover was actually a series of feasts. There are seven Jewish feasts that God commanded His people to observe each year. Three of them occur during a one-week period that is called the Eight Days of Passover. These three feasts are The Feast of Passover, The Feast of Unleavened Bread, and the Feast of First Fruits. Since the Feast of Passover is first, it serves as a kick-off to the spring festival season, and so all three feasts fall under the umbrella title of The Eight Days of Passover. You can read about all seven feasts in Leviticus 23.

The Feast of Passover itself is a feast that occurs each year on the Jewish calendar on the 14th of Nisan. This is typically in March or April of a given year on our calendar. Passover involves food. There is a traditional Passover Seder, or meal, that is served and is highly symbolic of the exodus from Egypt under Moses. The point of the Passover Seder is to remind God's people that He is the one who meets their needs. The Hebrew people hungered for freedom, and God delivered. When the angel of death came sweeping through Egypt, he passed over God's people who followed the command to kill a lamb and smear its blood on their doorposts. Faith and reliance on God instead of self will save you.

The second feast is the Feast of Unleavened Bread and it occurs the day after Passover on the 15th of Nissan and runs for seven days. This feast also involves food. During this time, God's people are commanded to eat only unleavened bread. The reason for this unusual command relates to the haste with which the Hebrews fled Egypt after the night of Passover. They were in a hurry. They did not even have time to let their bread rise, thus it had to be *unleavened* bread. It is, once again, a feast that celebrates God's provision for their needs. Even today, Jews take God's command to eat only unleavened bread very seriously to the point of cleaning their houses, boiling their utensils, and washing their clothes; all to ensure that no leaven can be found.

The last of the spring feasts involves food as well and is called the Feast of First Fruits. It occurs on the 16th day of Nissan, which is the second day of the week-long Feast of Unleavened Bread. In early Jewish culture, this was the day that the spring harvest would be celebrated and the people would give the first portion, or the first fruits, of their harvest as an offering to God. As is the case with the other two feasts, the idea is that everything we have comes from God. We seek God first to satisfy all our hungers. As a sign of recognition and gratitude, we give back to God.

These feasts are powerful symbols of a people who are hungry and who know it. They turn to God for all their provision and God delivers. He feeds the hearts, souls, minds, and strength of His people. He does this in response to their love for Him. Apart from a love for God, a love where we recognize that He is the one and only true and living God and the only one who can satisfy all our hungers, we are left to feed ourselves. When we attempt to feed ourselves, one way or another, on one or more levels, we *will* become the boiling frog in the kettle.

Chapter 4 – Alone

Okay, I admit it, I'm a sci-fi buff. I was raised on *Star Trek* re-runs (that's the original series) and I am of the generation of the original three *Star Wars* films. It's probably my older brother, Grant's, fault. He was a *Star Trek* guy too, and being one to look up to an older brother, I fell in, lock and step. I have always had a fascination with "space, the final frontier." There is something magnetic about the mystery of what might be "out there." As a kid, I used to love to watch old episodes of *The Twilight Zone,* and my favorite episodes were the ones with aliens. I am obviously not alone in my fervor. Hollywood has made big bucks on movies that play off of the possibility of life in the cosmos. Every year there seems to be another potential blockbuster waiting to tickle our imaginations with the idea of life in places other than Earth. Whether it is another *Star Wars* or *Star Trek* film, a remake of *Invasion of the Body Snatchers,* or something new all together, there is money to be made in aliens. Just look at the publishing industry. There is a whole genre of fiction dedicated to *science* fiction. Go into any bookstore and you will see that science fiction occupies its own very large section of square footage.

Is Anyone Out There?

I think the fascination people have with science fiction is the very real hope that there is more science than fiction going on. That there is a possibility of life somewhere else in our universe. I believe that many, many people want there to be life on other planets, and this desire is fueled by an ingrained and even deeper desire to not want to be alone. Surely we aren't the only ones out here in space. We can't be alone, can we? These sentiments are driven by our need for companionship. We just can't stand the thought of being alone on an individual level, much less a planetary level. If there is life out there, that means we aren't alone, and *that* gives us comfort.

Three, Two, One, Contact!

In 1997, the late Carl Sagan's 1985 novel, *Contact*, was released as a major motion picture starring Jodie Foster and Matthew McConaughey. This was intellectual sci-fi at its best. The story surrounds Foster's character, who has devoted her life to the search for extraterrestrial life. She is convinced we are not alone. In her own words, "If we are alone, then that's a whole lot of wasted space out there." She spends her days and nights listening to cosmic radio waves, looking for a message from our "neighbors" next door in space. As fate would have it (this is Hollywood, remember?) she stumbles across a complex message sent to us from other intelligent life. I won't spoil the story, but it turns out that the message earth receives is actually a response to our own television and radio broadcasts that have been and still are traveling through space.

The whole premise is interesting: The idea that radio signals, traveling at the speed of light, are emanating from our planet and could potentially be received by alien life, which would then return to us their own message. This isn't fiction either. People are taking this stuff very seriously. SETI (The Search for Extra-terrestrial Life) is an organization that is dedicated to just this kind of work. Founded in 1984, SETI employs 150 scientists, educators and support staff. The organization's website spells out its mission statement: *The Mission of the SETI Institute is to explore, understand and explain the origin, nature and prevalence of life in the universe.*

SETI has landed millions of dollars in support from companies and entities such as NASA, Hewlett Packard, Sun Microsystems, the Department of Energy, and many others. In the organization's own words, *"We believe we are conducting the most profound search in human history — to know our beginnings and our place among the stars."*[1]

To Boldly Go Where No Man Has Gone Before...

SETI is convinced we aren't alone. So convinced, they are spending millions scouring the cosmos looking for life. The idea is one based on probability. The universe is infinite, we are told. If this is true, then in an infinite universe, all probabilities are actual because all possibilities will be fulfilled at some point. If life evolved here, then it has to have evolved somewhere else. But there is a flaw in this way of thinking. If we carry the idea of infinite possibilities to its logical conclusion, that would mean that somewhere, out there, there is another me, and another you. It would even mean that this very book is floating around out there on another planet. Hopefully it's a bestseller! But of course, this is ridiculous.[2]

Nevertheless, the search for life goes on. Let me point out that when we speak of life on other planets, we are not necessarily speaking of *intelligent* life. There is a huge difference between a dandelion and a human being. Just because we might find water or even a microbe of life on another planet, we are still a long way from being able to have a conversation with an alien being.

Let's talk about this whole idea of sending and receiving radio waves as a way to establish contact with alien life, and thus prove that we are not alone.

In 1995, a couple of guys, Michel Mayor and Didier Queloz of the Geneva Observatory, discovered a planet orbiting a star called 51 Pegasi. This star is 45 light years from earth, located in the constellation Pegasus. A radio signal beamed at 51 Pegasi and sent out in 2008 would not reach that star until 2053. If there is life, and if it is intelligent life, and if they have advanced to the point that they can receive our message, and if they can understand it, and if they send a message back, the soonest we would receive our return letter would be 2098. Not exactly the instant communication we are used to. From a cosmic perspective, 51 Pagasi is just next door. In 1974, the strongest man-made signal ever transmitted was aimed and sent toward the Great Cluster of the constellation Hercules. Even optimists will admit that because of the limitations of time and distance, it could take millions of years for intelligent life to receive such messages, and by the time we receive a reply, their civilization may have become extinct.[3]

All Ahead, Warp Factor 6...

As much of a barrier that exists in radio wave communication with extraterrestrial life, there is an even greater barrier when it comes to physical travel. Movies and books portray space as teeming with life, and travel between planets as no big deal. There are many, many people who seriously claim to have seen UFOs, and stories of alien abduction abound. I recently watched a special on the Discovery Channel on the Area 51 and Roswell, New Mexico alien crash site conspiracy. It can be easy to believe that aliens are popping in and out of orbit all the time.

But there are serious and real problems with the idea of space travel. As I already said, 51 Pegasi is one of the closest systems with another planet around it. We don't know if there is intelligent life there or not, but let's just say there is. Our only experience as a species with space travel was the Apollo missions. The Apollo space craft moved at a cookin' one-millionth the speed of light. That is really fast, but in terms of space travel, it is slow. It would take four million years for us to travel to the nearest star at that speed. It would take 45 million years to travel to 51 Pegasi which is "just around the corner." You'd need more then an extended weekend to make that trip.

If you could increase your speed to one-tenth the speed of light, it would still take you 450 years to make the journey. Half the speed of light still takes 90 years. These are all one-way tickets. At this point you've got to start talking about near light speed travel (unlikely for carbon-based life), suspended animation, and a whole host of other issues like fuel and food consumption. Others have gone even further to solve these problems by talking about "wormholes" and other theoretical gateways that would make space travel possible.[4]

As much as I don't want to believe it, (because I just love the thought of stepping into a transporter one day and beaming down to a planet to meet people who speak English,) I have to be intellectually honest and admit that for all practical purposes, we are *alone* in the universe. This whole talk about life on other planets and SETI and movies and aliens serves to illustrate a very important point. People feel alone and people don't like it. We want so bad to have companionship, to know that no matter who we are or where we may go, we really aren't alone.

Creation's Missing Link

Most people would never guess this about me, but I am an introvert. In my role as a pastor and educator, I am externally expressive and most people think this is how I am all the time. When I get in front of a crowd, it is like a switch is flipped inside of me and I take charge of the situation and go for it. But that is not who I am naturally. I don't want you to think that I'm faking it, though. It really is a natural thing for me to be *loud* and *expressive* and *forceful* when I am teaching or preaching, but those three words don't describe my default nature. The people who remember me as a teenager before I became a Christian will tell you that this is true.

I was the kid that sat on the back row in Sunday School. I was the one who looked down when a question was asked. I wanted to blend in. The thought of standing in front of a group of people terrified me. But once I became a follower of Jesus, all that changed. My ability to teach and preach is a gift from God. In fact, God gives all Christians what the Bible calls spiritual gifts.

Because of my introverted tendencies, I like to be alone. I cherish times when I can just be by myself to think and read and study. Even though I enjoy my alone time, I can only handle so much of it. When I am alone it never fails that I find myself thinking about my wife or my three kids. I have spent about three hours alone today working on this chapter, and my thoughts have drifted to them numerous times. I can't wait to get home and be around them. As much as my alone time means to me, I wouldn't want to live that way.

I think all of us at various times need to be alone. People can be very draining. Even the most extroverted person who actually draws energy from being with people needs a break at some point. Silence and solitude are important disciplines to maintain. But at our core, we are created as social beings and we *need* people.

The 2000 movie *Castaway*, with Tom Hanks, is a powerful illustration of this need. Hanks plays the character Chuck Noland who works for FedEx. On a fateful flight one evening, the FedEx plane he hops a ride on crashes over the ocean and Chuck is stranded on an island...alone. A major part of the story is the extent to which Hanks' character goes to create companionship. In an act of desperation and to maintain his sanity, Hanks takes a volleyball that has washed ashore and, using his own blood, paints a face on the ball and names it *Wilson* (after the company name printed on the ball). For several years, Wilson is Chuck's best friend. He talks with Wilson and shares his intimate thoughts with "him". When Chuck finally builds a make-shift boat in an attempt to get off the island, he takes Wilson with him, only to lose him in the ocean. In a moving scene, Chuck is seen crying out to Wilson, sobbing and agonizing over the loss of his "friend." You see, we simply aren't built to live life alone.

When God created the heavens and the earth, he paused at various stages along the way to make a statement about His handiwork. "And God saw that it was good." This phrase or a variation of it is used six times in the opening chapter of Genesis. God declared that the light was good. He declared that the vegetation was good, that the animals were good, that the sea life was good, and so on. But when we arrive at chapter 2, we see that God looked at all He had created and He saw one fault. Creation had a missing link. God declared that, "It is not good that man should be alone."[5] Can you believe that? God admitted something very critical about who we are as the Image of God. It is not good to be alone.

So what did God do?

He made Eve.

A helper.

A companion.

Because it is not good for the Image of God to be alone.

This is interesting. God and Adam were together in creation, but that was not enough. For those people who say, "All you need is God," they are wrong. God Himself declared it. As important as a relationship with God is, we need more. We need human companionship. Let's go a step further. I would say that as important as human companionship is, we also need God. As the Image of God, we need both. As we have seen in the first chapter, the relationship with both was shattered in the Garden of Eden.

In a very real way, when we commit any sin, whether it be eating the fruit that God said not to eat, or telling a lie to our spouse, what we are doing is saying that we don't need God, that we don't want Him. We declare that our way is better than God's way. "Just leave me alone, God!" is our cry. What does God do in response? He grants us our wish.

Home Alone

Have you ever seen the movie *Home Alone*? It's a great holiday movie. Our family has it on DVD and we watch it each Christmas season. A boy named Kevin is the central character. He's ten years old and like many ten year olds, he knows it all. There is a scene at the beginning of the movie where chaos is abounding in the home. Extended family has arrived and the house is packed full of people trying to get ready to leave the next morning for a Christmas vacation. During a frantic pizza supper, food gets spilled and Kevin gets blamed by the whole family. He blows his top and his mother escorts him upstairs, where he will spend the night. He defiantly tells his mother that his family members are jerks and that he wishes that they would all be gone when he wakes up in the morning. He thinks his life would be better if he was alone, and he makes sure his mother knows it. Kevin's mom looks him deadpanned in the face and says, "You had better be careful what you wish for, you just might get it." Of course, you know how the movie goes, whether you've seen it or not. Through a set of crazy and funny circumstances, Kevin really does get left home alone. His wish is granted.

This is exactly what God has done for us. Adam and Eve declared by their actions that they didn't need God, and so God sent them out on their own. History has repeated itself ever since. People today don't think they need God. Until they're alone. It doesn't take much alone time, though, before people begin to cry out to God. I can't begin to tell you how many times I have heard people, in anguish over the circumstances of their life, ask me where God is.

"It's like He doesn't hear me."

"It's as if He's not there."

"Where is God when I need Him?"

Have you ever been there? Life is going along pretty well. You're doing well on your own. You're pretty self-sufficient and don't need much, right? Then all of a sudden you get a call from school and your daughter has fallen and hit her head. Or your yearly physical exam reveals something that needs to be looked at more closely. Maybe it's a reorganization of the company announced by your employer. Life has this funny way of slapping us in the face when we least expect it. At that point we really need God.

I've always thought it was interesting how in the days and weeks after a national crisis people will flock to church. People who never go except at Christmas and Easter. You know, the holly and the lily crowd. 9/11 is a perfect example. On that fateful day in 2001, the phones at our church began to ring almost immediately. People wanted to know if they could come pray. Sure. We opened the worship center and made it available. And people came. Why? They were looking for answers. They were looking for God.

But what if you couldn't find God? I mean, truly couldn't find Him. What if you really were all alone and no amount of prayer or Bible reading revealed Him to you? As I have mentioned, there have probably been times in all our lives, and you may be in one of those times right now, where God just feels absent. God really isn't absent, though. He really is there despite what you may feel.

But…what if, just what if God were truly and completely, all of a sudden, gone? And no matter how hard you tried or how loudly you called, God just simply wasn't there. That, my friend, is what I would call *hell*. You see, hell is real and it is a place where God, in the most fullest sense possible, grants to Man his wish. To be forever and completely rid of God. To be alone. For all that hell may be in terms of fire and punishment, hell is best defined as the absence of God.

Your Local "Community" Center

You see, it really isn't good for Man to be alone. We need community. The word community means to *commune*. All people have a need to commune with each other and they have a need to commune with God. Now here's the great part. Jesus himself, at the direction of God, has established Community Centers all over the world where this can happen. These Community Centers are located in every country. In the United States, they are located in every state, county, and city. In fact, most cities have multiple Community Centers in them. They are called churches.

A church is a place where, on a very small level, you can return to Eden. A place where you can commune with God, and where you can commune with others who are seeking to connect with God. I know what you might be thinking. "Man, that sounds great, but it sure is idealistic, most churches I know have problems." It is true that churches are far from perfect and some of them have real and significant problems.

This is because a church really is nothing more than people, held together by their common love and devotion to Jesus Christ. Since we as people are the disfigured Image of God, the church is going to look disfigured as well. But it is a starting point. In fact, it is *the* starting point, and the hub of our journey to recover the Image of God in us.

At the church I pastor, we have adopted three words that explain who we are as a church. These three words serve as sort of a purpose statement. They are a track that we run all our ministries on. When someone comes to our church, we walk them down this track of purpose with great intentionality. The three words are:

Belong.

Believe.

Become.

We exist as a church to help people belong, believe, and become. I don't think there is anything too terribly original about these words. You can even Google these three words and get numerous hits from other churches that use them as well. Let me tell you what they mean to *us*.

Everyone needs to belong. We all have a need to be on the inside and not the outside. Ever been on the outside of a group? Sure you have, and it's not fun, is it? As a species, we are great at drawing boundaries that divide us. Democrat or Republican. Ford or Honda. Mac or PC. You get the idea. Every time we do this, someone is in and someone is out. That's what makes the "clique" so appealing, not everyone can get in, and if *we* are the ones that are in, we feel special. In contrast, if we are on the outside, we feel rejected. But God is different. Jesus cries out to "all who labor and are heavy laden, and I will give you rest."[7] I think that when Jesus says *all*, he means *all*. There is no exclusivity.

I get frustrated when I hear secularists criticize Christianity as an exclusive religion because we insist that Jesus is the *only* way to heaven. How dare we suggest that the Buddhist is wrong. That Islam is based on error. That Hindus have it wrong. How pretentious is Christianity for declaring itself to be the *only* religion to have it right.

This makes me mad because it is simply wrong to say that we as Christians are exclusivists. Yes, Jesus is the only way. Yes, you will not make it to heaven without him. But here's the deal: Jesus' gift of eternal life is free to *anyone* who wants it. It doesn't matter how much money you make, what country or religion you were born into, what your political persuasion is, what your job is, etc. If you, whoever you are, want Jesus, you can have him. That, my friend, is inclusive, not exclusive.

Can you sense that I am passionate about this? The church is a place where you can belong. This is so important because we recognize that people are alone, and at their core they don't want to be alone. They want to commune with God and with others. Church is where and how this happens.

But at my church, we are not content to leave it at belong. If all we are is a place where people belong, then we are nothing more than a social club. There has to be more. And more is *believe*. We want to walk you to the point where you believe that Jesus is who he says he is, that he loves you and died for you. We want you to believe that you can only have real life when you surrender your life to him. The gift he gives when you do this is eternal life in heaven when you die.

Even that is not enough. The sad truth is that most churches stop at belong and believe. The really exciting things begin to happen when you *become*. At my church, we want you to become a fully devoted follower of Jesus Christ. This means you are actively involved in worshipping God on a consistent basis, both privately and corporately. It means that you are plugged into Bible study. And it means that you have found a place to serve God and the world through the church.

When worship, Bible study, and service come together, you have what is called a disciple of Christ.

I hit only briefly on the last two words, believe and become, because for the purposes of this chapter, I want to focus on the first word, belong. I want you to notice the order of our three words of purpose: belong, believe, become. The order is important, even critical to who we are as a church. We want people to know that no matter who they are, or how messed up they are, that they can *belong* at our church.

There are some who will take exception to this. The truth is that in many churches, if they used these three words, *believe* would come before *belong*. I think this is one of the biggest problems that churches face today. They want people to believe first and *then* they can belong. Oh, they may sing songs like *"Just As I Am,"* but what they mean is come *"Just As We Are."* In too many churches, if a person with tattoos, an eyebrow ring, and flip-flops walks into a church, it is clear that they do not belong. While it may not be said (but many times it will be), the message is sent loud and strong, to go clean up and then you can be a part of "us." And you know what happens? That person who stumbled into church lost, hungry and alone, leaves the way he came in. How utterly tragic. At this point, the Community Center has failed. That, dear reader, is exclusivity; you've got to meet the requirements of the club in order to join. Pay your dues and you can get in. You've got to lose the earring, cover the tattoo, and don the sport coat with a crest on the pocket. It makes me, as a pastor, sick.

To combat this attitude, we have become very intentional at my church about *belong*. All sinners welcome! As Max Lucado proclaims in the subtitle of one of his bestselling books, *God loves you just the way you are, but He refuses to leave you that way. He wants you to be just like Jesus.*[6]

What About Bob?

I met Bob one Sunday morning as I was walking into our worship center for our second service of the day. He looked nervous as he was sitting in our greeting area. I introduced myself and he did the same, and then Bob quickly added, "Man, I'm nervous!" He sort of caught me off-guard because most people I meet aren't that honest about their insecurities. I asked why he was nervous and he told me that this was the first time he'd been to church since he was 15. Now in his mid-20s, Bob was back in church, and I suspect that the reason he was nervous was because he was afraid he wouldn't fit in, that he'd made a mistake by coming to church, and that he just didn't belong. I told Bob I was excited that he was checking us out and that I wanted to see him after the service and find out how it went.

Sure enough, after we were done with the worship service, Bob found me and he had a big grin on his face. "Man, *that* was awesome!" were the first words out of his mouth. I asked him if he'd come back and he said yes. Bob has been a regular for some time now. His story is very intriguing to me, and the more I find out the more I understand why he felt so nervous that first Sunday, why he was afraid he wouldn't fit in.

You see, Bob's story goes like this (and this is the Reader's Digest version). Bob had hooked up with a stripper several years before. They lived together, she got pregnant and had a little girl. After the baby was born, the stripper wanted out so she hit the road. Bob has been left as a single dad to raise his little girl by himself. Bob has since entered a relationship with another woman and they are now living together, his daughter being two years old at this time. This is the life Bob was living when he stepped into our church for the first time.

I just wonder how many churches would, in no subtle fashion, turn Bob, his live-in girlfriend, and his two year old daughter away. "Go get married and clean up and then you can be a part of us." Here's the problem: In the world that Bob lives, he doesn't even know that it is outside of God's will to be living with a woman outside of marriage. All he knows is that in spite of all his efforts to get life right, he has made a mess of things. He feels alone and he needs and wants help. So he comes to church looking for the answer.

This is exactly why *belong* is so important. Bob needs to know that he fits and that church is a safe place to figure out God. Because I know that he needs to change some things in his life in order to receive God's best and to know God fully, it is my job to help him, not send him off on his own to figure it out.

It's funny (and sad) how we categorize and label sin in such a way as to exclude certain kinds of people, people that aren't like us. Do I really want to go around giving out sin questionnaires to the people who come to my church just so I can send them away to "clean up" first? No way. If I did that, there'd be no one to worship with on Sundays. I wouldn't even qualify to attend! That's because no one is perfect. We are all sinners. That includes people who've been in church their whole lives and people who've been out for ten years or more like Bob. We are all in the same boat. We've all got our stuff to deal with. And we all belong.

One More Lonely Story

Wanda walked into my office on a Thursday afternoon. She had requested an appointment, saying that she needed to get some things off her chest. As Wanda and I sat and talked, she began to tell me her story. She had actually grown up at our church and, in fact, still had family in the church. But as early as her teenage years, she began to slip away from an interest in God and church and became much more interested in boys and booze. Sitting in my office on this, a beautiful winter afternoon, Wanda, now in her mid-50s, showed all the physical signs of a rough life.

Wanda confessed that alcohol eventually led to drugs, and the combination eventually led to a life of addiction. Wanda met a man who really was not interested in God and the two began to build a life together that included children and all the outward markings of what the world would call success. Wanda has battled her addiction, spending thousands of dollars and entering numerous treatment programs. At present, the drugs are gone and she is now a recovering alcoholic actively involved in Alcoholics Anonymous.

Today, Wanda has everything. A nice home, a dedicated husband, and as much disposable income as any person could want. But yet, Wanda is sitting in my office on this particular day explaining to me that she is lacking something very important in her life. She feels alone.

Wanda has found her way back to church. Our church, the church of her youth. Since I am the pastor, she has found her way to my office and she wants to know where God is and why He seems so far away and absent in her life.

As I speak with Wanda, I begin to ask her about whether or not she has ever given her life to Jesus Christ. Oh, yes, she says, and she goes on to explain a detailed conversion experience as a child that included baptism into the Body of Christ.

So how is it possible that a Christian can be so alone and that God can seem so absent? Is she really a Christian? Did it just not "take" when she was a kid, and does she need to get "saved" again?

Wanda's Wall

Wanda's story is so common. Oh, the details and names change, but the gist is the same. "I used to be close to God, I slipped away, and now no matter what I do, I can't seem to get back to Him. I'm alone." Let me tell you a secret…I've even known committed Christians, people who go to church every week and give, study their Bibles, serve, do all the right things, who at times in their life will admit that God just seems to disappear. They feel so alone. If I am going to be transparent, I will admit that even I have been there; I have experienced that feeling of total aloneness. I am not sure if there is a darker feeling than that feeling. The feeling that God is simply not there. The feeling is compounded when you hear others talking about how alive their relationship is with God. How He speaks to them and what He showed them this week. They seem so close to God and yet you feel so far. You want what they have, but no matter what you do, you can't seem to seize it.

I spent a great deal of time with Wanda revisiting her salvation experience. This was important to me because I had to dig out what actually happened to her way back those many years ago. What exactly was her decision as a child as it related to Jesus? Many times, people will make a move toward God just because it seems the thing to do. This is common among people, especially children and teens. Peer pressure can be a powerful mover in the lives of all of us. In fact, in my own life, that is exactly what happened. When I was 11 years old, at a children's camp in Siloam Springs, Arkansas, I walked the aisle because my friend Jerome told me to. Everyone was doing it. "Go ahead," he said, "you go too. I'll even go with you." So I did. I said the prayer. I went home, told my parents and got baptized. But I will tell you today that when I was 11, I made no decision to consciously turn my life completely over to Jesus Christ. I just didn't want to be *alone* in not doing what everyone else was doing. This led to some real confusion later on in my early teenage years when God really began to move in my heart. I eventually waded through all the confusion and finally made a real commitment of my life to Jesus when I was 14.

So it was important to me to find out what really happened to Wanda. As she shared her story, I became convinced that she had indeed given her life to Christ as a young person. I came to the point that I had no doubt that I was speaking to a fellow believer in Jesus. The discussion moved to how a Christian can feel so alone in terms of God's presence.

First, I emphasized to Wanda that since she had given her life to Christ as a child, that she was, in fact, still a Christian today. But there was a barrier. For Wanda, that barrier was a lifetime of drug and alcohol abuse. "How can God still love me?" she asked. "How can He still care about me?" I told Wanda that Jesus had died for her long before she was ever born or had ever committed any sin or offense against God. She agreed. This is critical to understand. Jesus loved you and died for you *before* you ever committed a single sin. This means that your sins, all your sins, were paid for by Christ at His death some 2000 years ago.

Jump ahead to *now* and to *you*. When you give your life to Christ, when you accept His sacrifice for you, all your sins are miraculously forgiven, *all* your sins. It is a once for all decision. Now you live a life where you attempt to be sin-free. But we still have nuclear fallout to deal with. Our DNA is still prone to sin. So we sin. I don't know a single Christian who doesn't, on some or even many levels, continue to sin. But the difference now is that our sins are forgiven. Does this give us a license to go out and just do what we want, to "sin-it-up?" As Paul would say, "Certainly not!"[6] If you do, there will be consequences. I'm not talking about losing your salvation or about the consequence of spending eternity in hell. No, if you are a Christian, you are secure, heaven is your destination. The consequence I am talking about is the one with which Wanda was living. The consequence of being alone.

Convinced of her salvation, the second thing I did with Wanda was share with her the illustration of a wall. Once we give our lives to Christ, Jesus is with us and in us. Nothing can change that. But there is the DNA problem of sin. As we continue to sin in little and big ways, what we do, in effect, is begin building a wall one brick at a time. I explained it to Wanda like this. Let's say that as she and I are talking in my office, I just reach down and lay a brick on the floor between us. No big deal, right? It's just a brick, one brick. Now let's say that one at a time, I put down a row of bricks. Just one row, one brick high. More obvious but still not a big deal. We can continue talking and sharing stories. We can even exchange items such as me giving her a bottle of water if she is thirsty. But I continue to lay more bricks, row after row. Any one brick by itself is not that obvious. In fact, as a wall begins to form, one *more* brick seems more and more like less of a big thing. I mean, it's just one brick in a whole wall, right? And that's the thing. No matter how few bricks there are, or how many bricks there are, one brick *never* seems like a big deal. But eventually, there will be a barrier, a wall. The exchange of items will become difficult and the ability to talk will be compromised.

At some point, we will still be able to hear each other, but no longer see each other. When eye contact is cut off, we have lost a critical part of the communication process. When we can't see facial expressions and body language, we are left to fill in the gaps on our own. It is possible, and even likely, that I will misunderstand Wanda, or she, me. Eventually we will have a wall that runs the length of the room and the height of the ceiling. Then comes that all-important moment when that one last brick is placed to cover the only remaining gap in the wall. When that brick is laid, all communication is lost. Oh, you might be able to tap or pound on the wall in an effort to get the attention of the one on the other side, but unless things change, what happens is that more bricks are laid and we begin working to double the thickness of our wall. So it goes, on and on, brick after brick.

Now here is the deal, and don't miss this. Have Wanda and I geographically moved away from each other? No. We are both still sitting in the same room exactly the same distance from each other as when we began our conversation. The only thing that has changed is the presence of a wall. And the wall makes all the difference in the world. For even though we may still be a matter of a few feet from each other, we are, in effect, *alone*.

This is exactly what we do with God. And this is exactly what Wanda had done with God. I told Wanda that after her decision to let Christ into the room of her heart as a child, she then proceeded to spend a lifetime building a wall between her and Him. As a result, it is only natural that she should feel alone, as if God just isn't there. I then asked Wanda the following question: How do you tear down a wall? Her answer (and I think she was starting to get it), *one brick at a time*. Just as it took years to build the wall, it will take years to tear it down.

As you are reading this chapter, you fit into one of two categories. Either you are not a Christian, or you are. If you are not a Christian, meaning that you have never committed your life to Jesus Christ, then you really are alone. God is far away and He has nothing to do with you. Those feelings of aloneness are legit because you *are* alone.

If you are a Christian and you have found yourself alone, and I mean truly alone (more than you're just having a bad day), what has happened is that on some level, to one degree or another, you have put down bricks between you and God by way of continual sin. What you need to do is begin knocking out bricks. As you do, you will eventually begin to hear and feel the thumping of God against the wall. You will have that sense that you really aren't alone. But don't stop yet! Keep going, keep knocking out bricks. Eventually, you will begin to hear the voice of God again. His voice will grow louder and louder and clearer and clearer. Then you will reach a point where you knock a brick down and you see God again and feel the warmth of His presence. As you continue to work (and depending on how big your wall is, this could take a lifetime), you will eventually find your-self sitting across from Jesus, enjoying a conversation and basking in the joy of his very presence.

Theologically, this is called *confession*. We don't confess as Christians in order to re-secure our place in heaven. As I said, once you invite Jesus into your life, he forgives all your sin: past, present and future. But confession is impor-tant because it is that process by which we remove those bricks that cut us off from God and keep us from hearing His instruction for our lives and receiving the blessings that He is waiting to hand us.

As the old saying goes, "confession is good for the soul." Amen and amen.

Chapter 5 – Pawn

Lost, hungry and alone. This is the nuclear fallout of sin. This is the disfigured Image of God. This is you and me. This is us. It is almost time for the Intermission, but before we take that break, I want to address one other aspect of our place in God's creation as the Image of God. These will be deep waters that I am going to wade into over the next several pages. I want to address one of the most complex and difficult issues in all of Christianity. I want to talk about evil and suffering.

Whole books have been written on the issue of evil and suffering and its place within Christian theology. I will admit that this is a big problem for those of us who believe in one all-powerful, all-knowing, all-loving God. The problem goes like this: If God is so powerful and loves us so much, then why are there so many bad things happening in the world all the time?

As I write this chapter, we are only four days removed from a cyclone that leveled the nation of Myanmar and killed over 40,000 people. Can you imagine that? 40,000 people. Just this morning I was browsing the news headlines on *Yahoo!* and I saw that an earthquake in China has killed 12,000 people. Before I left the house, I read in the *USAToday* where a woman in Colorado Springs was leaving Target yesterday and a guy hit her on the head with a brick, tied and duct taped her up, threw her in his truck and took off. The police caught him because she was able to manage a call to 911.

So what's up with all this evil? Where's God? Why does He allow typhoons and earthquakes to kill thousands? Where was He when this woman was clobbered with a brick? We're still wondering how He could let planes fly into buildings on September 11, 2001. I know many people for whom this is *the* issue that keeps them from God. They simply want nothing to do with this kind of God. As I said, these are deep and treacherous waters we will be exploring in this chapter. But I don't think I could do any exposé on who we are as the Image of God if I ignored this issue. So, with that said, grab your wetsuit and flippers and let's dive deep!

Back in the Garden

It really does go all the way back to the Garden. Our search for an understanding of evil and suffering starts, of all places, in the beginning. Remember the snake? The one that had a conversation with Eve and convinced her that *she* was more important than *He* (that's God, not Adam)? We saw in chapter 1 that this snake was really the great Lucifer, archangel of heaven, the fallen one, now Satan. But Satan's role and interference in the affairs of mankind did not end in Eden. Oh no, that really was just the beginning of all his meddling. You see, Satan *is* real.

There are many people who don't like to think this way. Not only is it scary, but all this talk about Satan and demons force us into a realm where most people have very limited knowledge. When we don't know things, we tend to avoid them. Of course, this is just how Satan wants it, to be "under the radar."

I want you to listen to me, dear reader, and listen carefully. Satan is not only real, but he is active, and he has a host of hellish beings at his disposal. He is organized. He has a strategy. And he knows you and me better than you may think. He is motivated out of pure hatred toward the God who kicked him from his self-appointed throne in heaven. His task is to disrupt God's plan and purpose for your life. To not only disfigure, but to ultimately destroy the Image of God. War has been declared, and you and I are the targets.

I do not say all of this to frighten you or to sensationalize the content of these pages. I speak the way I do here because far too many people, Christians and non-Christians alike, are so ignorant in these matters that when they are touched by the evil of this world, they end up not only blaming the wrong side, but they miss God's hand in the midst of tragedy.

Basic Training 101

Let's begin with a primer in spiritual warfare. The spiritual realm is occupied by two opposing forces. On one side there is God and his heavenly host of angelic beings, and on the other side is Satan, the rebel of heaven, and his demonic horde. Most people I know don't have a problem believing in the existence of God and even angels, but when you start talking about the "devil" and "demons," you can get some unusual looks. This just shows how far our mindset has drifted from that of a biblical worldview.

The Bible not only teaches that the people of God will experience suffering in this life, but we can also expect to be touched by evil itself. In fact, Jesus taught that much of the human suffering we experience is directly linked to spiritual war, specifically demonic influence. Most Christians I know have never thought of it this way. They have always just assumed that we get sick and suffer because that's just part of being human, or because God doesn't care about them. But know this, Satan is mentioned 47 times in the Bible, and demons are mentioned 69 times. The press they get in God's Word is just proof that they are real and active.

Point Man Jesus

Imagine that you're 18 again. You graduated from high school just six months ago and you do not know what to do with your life, so you decide to let Uncle Sam make you "Army Strong." Today when you woke up in your tent you began your day by shaking the dust off your fatigues and boots. "Woke up" is a relative term because nobody sleeps that well in the sultry heat of the desert. You check your weapon and step out of your tent as the sun is still invisible to the new day.

Welcome to Iraq.

Today is different. You are scheduled to patrol a restless neighborhood in Baghdad located outside the Green Zone. A reporter was kidnapped there last week and the word is that terrorist activity is on the rise. Your job today is one you have dreaded. Today, you are the Point Man. The leader of the patrol. The one out front. When you stop, they stop. When you go, they go. If someone decides to take a shot, you are the first to get hit. The decisions you make today will impact the lives of seven other soldiers.

In a spiritual and real sense, Jesus was the Point Man when he walked on this earth. He was out front, followed by 12 men. Just as he tangled with the human agencies of the Pharisees and the Sadducees, he also battled spiritual forces. The four Gospels are the accounts of Jesus' life on earth. They also contain information on his engagement with the enemy forces of Satan's army. We've already seen in chapter 3 how Jesus went head-to-head with Satan himself, but Jesus also engaged Satan's infantry…they are known as demons. The accounts are fascinating and tell us much about how they relate to our own contact with evil and suffering.

In Matthew 12:22, Jesus has an encounter with a man that we are told was oppressed by a demon. Notice the language of the account in this gospel, and particularly the demon's relationship to this man's physical suffering,

Then a demon-oppressed man who was blind and mute was brought to him, and he healed him, so that the man spoke and saw.

The man was blind and mute, but after Jesus expelled the demon, the man could see and speak again. Am I saying that all people who are mute or blind are demon afflicted? No. What I am saying is that *this* man was, and that it isn't crazy to assert that there is a connection between spiritual conflict and human suffering. Let's look at another example.

Matthew records in chapter 17 an encounter that Jesus had with a man whose son suffered from epilepsy. Look at the account as it appears in verses 14-20:

And when they came to the crowd, a man came up to him and, kneeling before him, said, "Lord, have mercy on my son, for he is an epileptic and he suffers terribly. For often he falls into the fire, and often into the water. And I brought him to your disciples, and they could not heal him." And Jesus answered, "O faithless and twisted generation, how long am I to be with you? How long am I to bear with you? Bring him here to me." And Jesus rebuked him, and the demon came out of him, and the boy was healed instantly. Then the disciples came to Jesus privately and said, "Why could we not cast it out?" He said to them, "Because of your little faith".

Question: Do you believe the Bible or not? This is a pretty straightforward story. A boy suffers the affliction of epilepsy, the disciples try to "heal" him, but are unsuccessful. Then Jesus steps in, a demon comes out of the boy, and he is healed instantly. It seems clear that in this case, a demon was causing the condition of epilepsy. I think it should be pointed out that when the disciples inquired as to why they were unsuccessful in healing the boy, Jesus accused them of a lack of faith. I wonder at what point their faith was lacking. Could it be at the point of belief that human suffering could be demonically related?

Let's look at another case that is recorded in the gospel of Luke. In chapter 13, Jesus once again is playing the role of Point Man. One particular Sabbath day, Jesus was teaching in a synagogue to anyone who wanted to come hear him preach. We are told in verse 11 that a woman was present that day who had been afflicted with a "disabling spirit" for 18 years. She was horribly bent over and could not straighten up.

Now, what would we do with someone like that today? Think about it. We'd probably send them to therapy and maybe give them some vitamins to increase bone density. Would we ever even consider that something more might be involved? Well, Jesus did and we are told that he "freed" the woman of her disability and that immediately she was able to straighten up. What happened next is interesting. The religious elite began to criticize Jesus for healing this woman on the Sabbath, as if he was breaking the law. Jesus responded. Look at his words in verse 16:

> *"And ought not this woman, a daughter of Abraham whom Satan bound for eighteen years, be loosed from this bond on the Sabbath day?"*

Notice that Jesus gave full credit for this woman's debilitating condition to Satan himself. Jesus had no problem believing and teaching that evil does indeed play a role in human suffering. Jesus understood that there was a war going on and that people were being used for target practice. Not only did he enter the picture to bring triage to the wounded, but he put himself up against the firing squad, and took the bullet for you and me. Amazing, isn't it?

The gospel of Mark goes further. It indicates that these were not isolated incidents that we are talking about here, but that Jesus' spiritual encounter with demons at the point of human suffering was a common experience. Look at this passage from chapter 1, verses 32-34:

That evening at sundown they brought to him all who were sick or oppressed by demons. And the whole city was gathered together at the door. And he healed many who were sick with various diseases, and cast out many demons. And he would not permit the demons to speak, because they knew him.

We live in a culture today that simply lacks faith in these kinds of things. I believe that we are so sanitized in our thinking that there is no room for the supernatural. Oh, we are okay with God and the Holy Spirit, as I've already said, but when it comes to the darker side of spiritual conflict, especially when that darker side touches who we are as humans, our belief goes out the window. We'd rather send someone to therapy or medicate them rather than even consider the possibility of evil being involved.

Now let me clarify myself, because at this point I am fearful of being misunderstood. I am *not* saying that all human illness is related to demonic activity. What I *am* saying is that demons are real and active, and they do attack people physically at various times. Yes, it is good that we have medicine, doctors, and therapists, because I believe people do get sick just because people get sick. But please don't tell me it's crazy to assert that evil can play a role in human suffering. The passage above illustrates both. It says Jesus "healed many who were sick with various diseases, *and* cast out many demons." It is biblical to think this way, and I will go even farther to say that it is naïve at best and unbiblical at worst to say that evil plays no role in human suffering.

These are just four scenes from the life of Jesus where he encountered demons as they were inflicting people with various forms of disease and pain. I have counted 13 such incidents in all, just in the gospels, where we see demons and suffering directly linked together. The people during Jesus' day and Jesus himself had no problem thinking this way.

Let me point out that there are places in the world today to which you can travel where it is commonplace for people to think this way, that evil spirits afflict people. In fact, they think you're crazy if you *don't* see the link. Only in "civilized" Western society, where science rules and we teach our children with public dollars that there is no God, do we scoff at the notion of demonic activity and human suffering as going hand-in-hand. *We have elevated our thinking. We have shrugged off such superstitious hocus-pocus.* But the problem with our *elevated* and *advanced* way of thinking is that we are still human, and that means that we will suffer in this life. And when push comes to shove and we have our backs against the wall with our own human affliction, we want to blame someone. In the absence of a complete understanding of the battleground, that Someone that we blame becomes God.

Casualties of War

It is a fact of life. In war, people get hit and people get killed. We all know this is how it works. Two guys are riding along in a Humvee and all of a sudden they take fire. One guy gets it right between the eyes and the other guy escapes without a scratch. When the unhurt soldier gets back to base, he wonders why his friend was hit and not him. "It doesn't seem fair," he says to his fellow soldiers. "It's just war," is their reply. As I said, this is how it works in war. We don't question when a car bomb goes off in a convoy, taking out two vehicles and killing a dozen men, while leaving the rest of the convoy alone and untouched. Soldiers know that's just the nature of war. In war there will be causalities.

So why do we think it will be any different in a spiritual war? That's just it. I think most people don't realize that there is a spiritual war going on all around us. Everyday. The bullets are flying, the bombs are going off, and people are getting hurt and maimed. War is hell and if you've ever felt like your life was hell on earth, then you have tasted of the conflict that I am speaking about in this chapter. We need to adjust our thinking. That is why I spent the last several pages talking about Satan and demons and their influence over us in terms of human suffering.

Since we are in this war, that means that on any given day, when you rise from your bed and put on your clothes and step out of your house, you are stepping into the battle-field and you could get hit. Or your kids could get hit. Or your spouse. Or your parents. Do you hear me? It's a war! And there could be an RPG aimed at you right now. This is not hard to grasp in an earthly war, yet it escapes us on a spiritual level when we see our loved ones dropping all around us. We need to elevate our worldview to include not only the natural but also the supernatural.

My Personal War Story

Julie and I were married in June of 1992. I had just grad-uated from college the month before and we were so excited about starting our life together. Our wedding was in Denton, Texas and it was beautiful. Julie was the most stunning bride

I have ever seen. She took my breath away when she came walking down that aisle. I felt, and still do, like the luckiest man on earth. Ours was a storybook beginning. We ran off to San Antonio for our honeymoon, and then we were off to Baton Rouge, Louisiana, where Julie and I had both been hired by the Parkview Baptist Church to work on a church growth project.

We rented a one bedroom apartment, Julie enrolled at LSU in order to complete her last year of school, the ministry was going well, and we were making friends with other newlywed couples. We were eight months into our marriage.

Life was good.

And then it all changed.

Julie had gone to her OB/GYN for her yearly "routine" appointment. As part of the exam, the doctor was checking her neck. He discovered a lump in her throat area. "Probably no big deal," he assured her. Julie was 21 years old and very healthy. The chances it could be abnormal were slim to none, but the doctor thought it'd be a good idea to just get it looked at.

Her OB/GYN referred us to a colleague of his, a surgeon. He ran a scan on Julie's neck and the conclusion was that it was some kind of tumor. "Probably benign," he said. "You're young. The chance it could be cancerous is slim. We just don't see that in people your age." We had two options: a biopsy or surgery, to remove the growth. Since our insurance was very limited and biopsies weren't covered, and since Julie had no desire to have anything abnormal growing in her body, we opted to have the tumor removed.

It was supposed to be a routine surgery, around an hour. After two hours, I knew something was wrong. After four hours, the doctor came out and gave me the word.

Cancer.

At age 21, my new bride, my precious Julie, had just taken a bullet. She was now fighting cancer. I'll admit that being young and in our 20s was a help. We were really too naïve to fully grasp the gravity of it all. And things were moving quickly. They had removed the tumor and performed a biopsy in the operating room. That is when they determined that it was an aggressive form of thyroid cancer called follicular carcinoma. As part of the protocol for thyroid cancer, the doctor went back into Julie's neck and removed the rest of her thyroid gland. She would be on synthetic thyroid hormone the rest of her life.

In the days after her surgery, we were referred to an endocrinologist who would oversee the next phase of Julie's battle with her cancer. The first thing that needed to be determined was whether or not the cancer had spread beyond the thyroid gland. She would undergo low-dose outpatient radiation regardless, as a preventative measure to obliterate any remaining thyroid tissue left over by the surgery. Remaining cancer, however, would dictate a very aggressive approach to high-dose inpatient radiation. As a part of our visits, the doctor had told us that there was a good chance that high doses of radiation could maker her infertile. But she was young, right? Healthy, right? There's no way this would be the case. The stakes were high.

She underwent a series of body scans so the doctor could "see" the inside of her body and what might be going on. On the day of her final scan, she had gone alone to the clinic while I was at work. She was expecting to be scanned, and then to just go back to work until her next appointment, whereby we would get the results. I'll never forget the phone call. I was having lunch with the pastoral staff of our church when I heard Julie's frantic voice on the other end. She said that her doctor had come in to look at the scans as they came off the machine. What he saw was a "mass" of what looked to him like abnormal cells in the thyroid area. He told Julie to go home, pack a bag and go straight to the hospital. He had already called and made arrangements for immediate treatment with high levels of radiation. He was convinced that this could not wait.

Julie was panicked and wanted to know what to do. I asked her if the doctor was *sure* of himself in terms of what he was seeing on the scan. He said he was. I don't know why, because I know little to nothing about medicine, but something in me told me that the doctor needed to look again. I told Julie to see if the doctor would run one more scan before we agreed to this radical treatment. He was reluctant, but he agreed, saying he'd do it only if she'd go straight to the hospital from the clinic as soon as the scan was complete and the results were in. I jumped in my car and headed for the clinic.

When I got there, Julie was already being scanned. It was a process that, in the 90s, took around 45 minutes. I didn't know what to do. Things were moving so fast and I felt like I was possibly losing not only a future with kids, but maybe my wife. So I prayed. I don't think I have ever prayed as hard or as intensely for anything as I did for my wife that day. Julie eventually came out when the scan was complete and we embraced. And we prayed. And then the doctor came out.

He had a look of confusion on his face.

According to what he was looking at now, the new scan, there was nothing in her neck at all. That's right, nothing. I get chills even now as I relive those moments. "I've never seen anything like this," were the doctor's words. He had been so sure of himself. He had no explanation other than what he saw before was some "shadow" or "anomaly", maybe even a salivary gland that he'd mistaken for cancer. Julie and I knew different. At the time we saw it as a miracle, a healing. And surely it was. But today, I will go one further. You see, today, I certainly believe my wife was healed, but

I also think that evil had touched us that day. And so our healing was not only physical, but I think also it was very spiritual.

I think this sort of thing happens everyday all around us. I think that there are spiritual forces swimming around us on a constant basis. Forces that we cannot see, but that we see effects of on this world. Too many times, God gets the blame as if this is all one-sided, but there is another side. That is my point. In order to complete basic training, *spiritual* basic training, you've got to acknowledge the enemy.

Chess

I learned to play chess from my grandfather. My grandfather was pretty old by the time I came along, so he wasn't physically able to do much anymore, but his mind was sharp as a tack until the day of his death, and he was always up for a game of checkers or chess. I used to love to go over to his house. He would go to his room and pull out his very old chess board and the cigar box that held the wooden chess pieces. He'd dump them out, we'd set them up, and then we'd go at it. I never beat him. Not even once. And he never let me beat him. He was the best chess player I ever knew, a most formidable opponent. Because of my love for my grandfather, I learned to love chess as well.

My brother, Grant, got this three-dimensional chess set for Christmas one year and it was the coolest thing I had ever seen. It reminded me of that multi-layered chess game that Mr. Spock would play on *Star Trek* (I told you I was a sci-fi buff!). Three dimensional chess is very different from regular chess, but at its essence it's the same. There are two sides and you use the same pieces. The object of the game is the same: checkmate. If you've ever played chess before, then you're familiar with the various kinds of pieces: King,

Queen, Rook, etc. But there is a certain piece on the chess board that is considered disposable.

The Pawn.

Pawns are used for all kinds of things. They are used to block, trap, confuse, and basically muddle up the chess board. There are a lot of pawns, more than any other kind of piece, which is why they are generally considered to be disposable. Have you ever felt like a pawn? Just kind of muddling around and knocked around by life. When evil and suffering touch your life, do you just feel disposable? I think that on the spiritual battlefield, it is easy to feel small and insignificant. The truth is, as God and Satan do battle, there are no unimportant pieces. Oh, to be sure, Satan doesn't care a whit about you and he would sacrifice you in a heartbeat to accomplish his ultimate objective of defeating God. It can seem at times like God doesn't care either. When you are lost, hungry and alone, it can seem like you are nothing more than a pawn in some galactic chess match.

Listen to me, there is *so* much more going on that you and I just don't see. Do you realize that at times you are actually the focal point of Satan's attention? Jesus warned Peter,

> *"Simon, Simon, behold, Satan demanded to have you, that he might sift you like wheat...."*[1]

And in the book of Revelation, we are told that Satan stands before God and accuses Christians day and night.[2] Imagine that. Satan knows you by name and he is doing battle over *you* before the throne of God. Sound too incredible? Do you think that you are just too insignificant to warrant such attention? Remember that Satan has been at work since the Garden of Eden, busying himself with disfiguring the Image of God.

Just imagine that in the cosmic chess match between Satan and God, the time has arrived for the next move. Both of their hands reach down and rest upon one piece on the board...you.

Playing Chess With Job

I have always been fascinated by the first chapter of the book of Job. In this one chapter of the Bible we get a glimpse into the spiritual world. We have a ringside seat for this chess match between God and Satan. What is described is a summary of all that I have been talking about in this chapter of the book you are holding. What we are given with Job is biblical real-life scenario. It is important to understand that what you will see in the book of Job chapter one is the kind of spiritual war that is played out even today, only the names have been changed. Instead of Job, it might be your boss, or your friend, or even you.

The chapter begins with the pawn...Job. We are introduced to Job in the first five verses and we learn that Job is a really good guy. He's married and has a lot of kids, seven boys and three girls. His quiver is full! We are told that Job is a straight-up guy. He loves and worships God, obeys God's laws, and tries to live a good, clean life. Job has been rewarded for his clean living. He has become a very successful herdsman with thousands of animals as part of his livestock. We are told that he loves his children deeply and prays for them every morning, offering sacrifices to God on their behalf. Job is a guy that does everything right. He has a good life.

Then the scene changes. Now we are in heaven. It is a normal, average day in the life of Job on earth, but the events unfolding in heaven are about to change Job's life forever. You see, Satan has singled out Job, he is about to ask for Job that he may sift him as wheat. As the scene opens, Satan, in all his swagger and arrogance, comes strutting into the throne room of God. Honestly, I can't do the words of the Bible justice at this point. You need to read it yourself:

> *Now there was a day when the sons of God came to present themselves before the Lord, and Satan also came among them. The Lord said to Satan, "From where have you come?" Satan answered the Lord and said, "From going to and fro on the earth, and from walking up and down on it." And the Lord said to Satan, "Have you considered my servant Job, that there is none like him on the earth, a blameless and upright man, who fears God and turns away from evil?" Then Satan answered the Lord and said, "Does Job fear God for no reason? Have you not put a hedge around him and his house and all that he has, on every side? You have blessed the work of his hands, and his possessions have increased in the land. But stretch out your hand and touch all that he has, and he will curse you to your face." And the Lord said to Satan, "Behold, all that he has is in your hand. Only against him do not stretch out your hand." So Satan went out from the presence of the Lord.*[2]

Do you see what I mean by fascinating? There are many misconceptions about spiritual warfare and Satan and his demons, and this passage clears them up. In these seven verses, we learn six truths about this war that God is fighting, and your and my place in it. I have preached these truths for years all across the country and every time I do people tell me that it changes their worldview. I want you to read the truths presented in the next few pages carefully. I believe they will change the way you look at evil and suffering and your place in this world.

Truth #1: Satan Has Access To Heaven

That's right, Satan has access to heaven. Every time I teach this truth, people look at me funny. That is because somehow people have developed a misconception about Satan and his place in the cosmos. I am not sure where this misconception comes from, but it is there. If you quiz the average person on the street, or even the average Christian in a church, they will probably tell you that they have always pictured Satan as being down in hell, plotting and scheming against God and His people. I will admit that I used to think this way. I used to view hell as sort of a base of operations for Satan. My view of hell was that it was Satan's "home," that he ruled this eternal place of torture, and that he was trying to pull as many victims into hell as possible. This is all wrong.

The truth is that hell is indeed real, but there is no one in hell yet, not even Satan. In fact, we are told that hell is a place prepared by God specifically for the punishment of Satan and his demon horde, as well as all those who reject Him. Hell is currently unoccupied and it will stay that way until the final judgment. Here's the thing about hell: once you get in, you don't get out. It's not a come-and-go type of thing. It is forever.

Since Satan has not been condemned to hell yet, that means he still has access to heaven. "But I thought God kicked Satan out of heaven," you may say. Yes and no. What God did, and we saw this when we looked at Isaiah 14 back in chapter one, is remove Satan from his office as archangel over heaven, and remove him as a resident of heaven. God cast him out. That does not mean that Satan does not still have *access* to heaven. That access is what we see in the book of Job. Verse 6 clearly tells us that Satan can visit heaven. The picture is one of God sitting on His throne, ruling over His creation, and as the angels (Job calls them the sons of God) were reporting to God the goings-on within the Kingdom, all of a sudden, a black wind comes sweeping through the Royal Chamber. Satan has arrived. He struts up to the throne of God and a conversation ensues.

Truth #2: Satan Has Access To Earth

You can almost see it. God and Satan staring each other down. The throne room of heaven so quiet you can hear a pin drop. The rejected and ejected archangel of heaven has returned. What once was beautiful is now deformed. The snake is rearing his ugly head once again in the face of God. God's voice breaks the silence, "Where have *you* been?"

"Oh, I've just been taking a walk on your precious little planet called earth. I've been checking it out and you won't believe what all I've seen," hisses the snake.

At this point, God reaches down and He places His mighty hand on a certain chess piece on the board. "Hey Satan, have you seen my man Job? I'm telling you there is none like him on the whole planet. He loves me intensely and he serves me and credits me with all the blessings of his life. What do you think about Job?"

"Well, of course, he 'loves' you, why wouldn't he?" retorts the snake. And he continues, "You've stacked the deck, God! You give Job everything: a wife, kids, money, land, cattle. The guy never even catches a cold! It's ridiculous...but I'll just *bet*..."

And there it is...the *wager*. The war is renewed and Job is the target.

"I'll just bet you God...I'll just bet that if you take away everything this guy has, he will curse you to your face."

There you have it. Satan is not in hell. If he's not in hell that means there are only two places that he can be: heaven and earth. And that is exactly where Satan is. He spends his time scouring the planet watching people. You and me. My

120

wife and kids. Your kids and your parents. He watches and waits and when he's ready, he makes his move to heaven where he asks for you. He stands before God's throne and accuses you day and night. Oh, yes, Satan has access to earth and he is like a lion roaming around seeking whom he can devour.[3]

Truth #3: God Controls What Satan Does

Notice that Satan wants God to do his dirty work for him. In verse 11, Satan challenges God, "But *you* stretch out *your* hand and touch all that he has..."(emphasis mine).

God will have none of it.

"Satan, if you want to go after Job, you'll have to do it yourself," says God. The text actually reads in verse 12 this way, "Behold, all that he has is in *your* hand" (emphasis mine). In essence, God says, "Don't make me the bad guy, Satan. This is your deal, your bet."

Notice what God does next. He puts a *limitation* on Satan. He tells Satan that he can touch anything or anyone in Job's life, but he is not allowed to touch Job's physical body, "Only against him do not stretch out your hand." Isn't that interesting? Satan is so big and bad and "in control," but God clearly is the one holding the real power here. God still controls Satan. In fact, I would go as far as to say that Satan can do nothing without getting God's permission first. This has to drive him crazy! The hatred and the rage must be exponentially building inside this creature of evil. He wants so badly to be where God is and to rule what God rules. He wants to be God.

Yet God still limits him.

Controls him.

Rules him.

And this leads right into our next great truth about spiritual warfare.

Truth #4: God Will Not Give You Anything You Can't Handle

It is so important that you don't miss this truth. This truth gets to the heart of this whole chapter. When bad things happen. When evil strikes. When your new bride of eight months is diagnosed with cancer, the question is "God, where are you?" You see, God may be *much* closer than you ever realized.

Then there's the follow-up question, "God, how can you do this to me?" But it may not be God. Oh, God is allowing it to happen, but there is a much bigger scenario playing out. You may not see it and that's okay, Job didn't see it either, at first.

If you read on into the book of Job, you will see that Satan hit Job hard. I mean really hard. On a normal average day, a day that started off with great promise, Job's world is rocked. In the course of perhaps just an hour, while Job is taking care of business, servants begin to arrive one after another with bad news.

"The Sabeans have attacked for no reason. They killed your servants and took the oxen and the donkeys," they cry.

"Fire fell from heaven and killed your workers and destroyed the whole sheep herd," they continue. And there's more, "The Chaldeans have attacked, taken the camels, and they left no one alive."

Then the worst news of all.

"Your children were together in their oldest brother's house for a feast. An F-5 tornado leveled the property and they're all dead. All ten of your children."

Let me ask you a question. What would you do with such news? You've just lost everything. And I mean everything. All your assets and all your children. All within an hour. What would you do? Remember, Satan has made a wager with God over what Job would do.

Job's response…

"Naked I came from my mother's womb, and naked shall I return. The LORD gave, and the LORD has taken away; blessed be the name of the LORD." In all this Job did not sin or charge God with wrong.[4]

Wow. Could you do that? I don't know if I could. Maybe now you can see why God singled Job out for recognition. You know, when bad stuff happens, so many times we want to know what we did wrong. Listen, when evil invades the serenity of your perfect life, it may not be a matter of what you are doing wrong, but of what you are doing *right*. At least that was the case with Job.

Here's the point I don't want you to miss: God knew Job. He knew Job better than Job knew himself. God was not about to give Job anything he couldn't handle. God works the same in your life. I don't know how bad you've had it, but I'd dare say none of us have faced what Job faced and to the level he faced it. God is in control and he will not give you more than you can take.

Truth #5: Satan Doesn't Really Care About You, He Hates God

Now Satan is really mad. He lost his bet. When you read on into chapter two, you will see what looks like a re-run from chapter one. Satan crashes heaven. God asks where he's been. Satan replies that he's been walking the earth. And then God just can't resist. "And what about Job?" He asks. And Satan blows his top.

"Skin for skin!" he shouts. "You didn't let me do enough to him," he complains. "*You* touch his body and I bet you the Kingdom that he will curse you."

God refuses to bite, "Do it yourself, but you can't kill him."

Once again, God limits. Satan leaves. The snake strikes. The venom courses deep. This time Job gets sick. Boils break out over his entire body. He is in emotional and physical misery. But Job continues to stand strong.

Now let me ask you, does Satan really care about Job? Oh, to be sure, he's the target and destruction is the goal, but does he really *care* about Job? The answer is "No." Satan doesn't give a rip about Job. Job is nothing more than a pawn. He is disposable. From Satan's point of view, the world is full of pawns just like Job that will serve only one purpose: *to hurt God*. You see, Satan despises God. He hates God. God is the goal, not Job. Satan will do anything and destroy anyone if it means that He can best God. He's been trying for thousands of years. Since the Garden to be exact. From the moment he was cut down, he's been working to cut God down.

His plan almost worked (he thought) when while walking to and fro on the earth one evening, he heard the distant cry of a baby. A baby boy at that. Someone's son. And not just any baby or just anyone's son, but God's Son. Satan concocted his greatest scheme yet. It took 33 years to play out, but evil is patient. It boils and festers until it pops. On the cross, the snake struck fast and hard with great ferocity.

And Satan won!

He killed God!

And heaven wept.

And Satan rejoiced.

And the demons danced and partied.

For three days…

…then Jesus crashed the party.

If you thought Satan was mad before, then the level of his hatred toward God now can no longer be measured. At every turn he has been thwarted and he has failed. But he is not one to give up. The chess match is not over. There are still moves to be made. And the only moves he has left involve you and me.

Truth #6: God Is Counting On You

One more question: What do you think would have happened if Job *had* cursed God? What if Job had decided that he had had enough, and that he wasn't going to take it anymore? What if he had torn his clothes, looked into heaven, raised his fist, and shouted, "Damn you, God! I have given everything to you. I have praised you and worshipped you and loved you. I have held nothing back. I've done everything you've ever asked of me. And how do you repay me? You strip me of all that I have. My children, my money, my land, all of it gone! What kind of God are you?! I curse you to your face!"

What do you think would have happened if this had been Job's response? I'll tell you what would have happened. Satan would have been back in heaven as quickly as God had kicked him out. He would have sprinted to the throne of God and with his chest puffed out he would have laughed in God's face, "I was right, God! I was right and *You* were wrong! I know Job better than you. What kind of God are you that doesn't even know His own slaves! You are pathetic! I knew I could run this whole thing better than you. I was right and you were WRONG!"

Any doubts that this would have been the result? What would God have done? I believe that He would have just cried. He would have cried because Job would have let Him down. You see, there really is a war going on out there, and *God is counting on you.*

I promise you, my friend, that as the bullets fly and the land mines go off, God is in control. I know it may not seem like it. You will have friends that will leave for work and never come home again. You yourself will take a few shots. It will seem at times like it is more than you can bear. But it's not. God knows your limits. Every person has limits, that's for sure, but God knows you better than you know your-self and I promise that He will never give you anything you can't handle. Remember this, in the midst of this war, Satan doesn't care about you, but God does. He cares about you... loves you...intensely. And He is counting on you. Don't let Satan laugh in God's face on your account. Be strong and courageous. Fight the good fight knowing that there is a crown of life promised to those who love Him.[5]

War kills. War maims. War *disfigures*. War is hell. If you have been hit and maimed and if the Image of God has been disfigured in the war, I have good news. Act 1 is over and it's time for an Intermission. The Intermission is where you take a break. It's where you find rest. It's where you prepare for Act 2. Don't miss the Intermission because the Intermission is where you will find God waiting to rescue you and airlift you to safety.

Intermission - The Image of God

Chosen

Intermission – Chosen

I remember the moment I became a Christian with crystal clarity. To coin a cliché, "as if it were yesterday." It was May 16, 1984 at 8:30 p.m. I was 14 years old. A preacher named Rick Stanley had rolled into town and was holding a youth revival at my church. Rick was the step-brother of Elvis Presley, which was pretty cool if you're 14, or any age for that matter. Rick had a powerful testimony of how God changed him. I was intrigued. As I shared in a previous chapter, I had already "walked the aisle" and been baptized when I was 11 years old at a children's camp. At the age of 11, it just seemed like the thing to do and my parents were proud of my decision. But now, three years later, going through the throws of adolescence and all that goes with it, things were different. I was beginning to see God in new ways, and my interest level in all things spiritual was growing.

May 16th fell on a Wednesday night in 1984. It was the last night of the revival. In an effort to get as many teenagers to come out, our church hosted a pizza pigout. So I went and ate pizza and then moved to the worship center to hear Rick's final sermon. I will admit that during the first three nights of the revival, my spirit had been very unsettled. I had this nagging sense that all was not right in my soul. But I kept thinking back to that "decision" I made three years earlier, and so I was okay, right?

As Rick preached that night, the sense that I was *not* okay grew and eventually became overwhelming. Of course, I would later chalk this up the Holy Spirit working on me. In the course of Rick's sermon I came to *know* that if my life were to end right then, I would be separated from God forever. I would go to hell. When it came time for the invitation, I was a brunette blur down the aisle, ready to give my heart and life to Jesus Christ. I was desperate for Jesus to forgive me and secure for me a place with Him for all eternity. I was also desperate to live my life fully and completely for Him.

They took all of us who came forward down to the choir room where counselors were prepared to answer all our questions. I told the two men who I was matched with that I wanted to become a Christian. They asked if they could lead me in a prayer and I said, "No. I want to do this myself." When I was 11, I had been "led" in a prayer and I wanted this experience to be different. I didn't want any issues about whether this was my decision or someone else's. I know a lot of people who are led in a prayer to accept Christ. There is nothing wrong with this. Many people don't have the right words to say at such a critical and emotional time, and it is very beneficial to have someone there to guide and help them with a prayer. Truthfully, the words are not the important part anyway, it's the attitude of the heart that really counts.

But I wanted to say my own prayer, and so I did. I asked Jesus to forgive me and save me. I asked him to come into my heart and live with me forever. I promised to live the rest of my life for him. And I thanked Jesus; I thanked him for saving me from myself and from hell. It was at 8:30 p.m. that this moment in my life became forever etched into my memory.

Which Came First...

With this 24-year-old story as the context, I now ask this question: Did I choose God or did God choose me?

And there it is. The classic debate that has raged within Christian circles for hundreds of years. To be sure, a choice was made in my life on May 16, 1984, but the issue is *who* did the choosing.

You may ask, "Why does it matter?" That's a good question, and to be honest, I don't think it matters as much as some people might think it matters. The important thing here is *you.* After all, if you'll remember, this is a book about you. At this point, it should be clear that you are in trouble. You are a sinner and because of this, you are lost, hungry and alone. To make matters worse, you are a pawn in a cosmic struggle between the spiritual forces of ultimate good and ultimate evil: God and Satan. Unless something changes, you are doomed. From this perspective what we are talking about in this chapter is very important, because we are, once again, talking about you.

I am taking time to write about this for another reason, too. Even though it is common for people to ask whether or not it really matters who does the choosing when it comes to salvation, I have also observed that once a person is a Christian, they are almost always interested in figuring out exactly *how* it happened. I have been in ministry for a long time now, and universally in every setting in which I have ministered, it is just a matter of time before the topic of Calvinism rears its head.

I Thought Calvin Was a Cartoon Character

I didn't even know about Calvinism or have a clue who John Calvin was until I went to college. During my sophomore year at Oklahoma Baptist University, I found myself drawn into the debate. It started by just listening to others talk about things like Calvinism, predestination and election. Regardless of the side someone took, they always seemed so passionate. There would be these really ugly arguments, usually followed by labels being thrown out ("label" is a nice word for name-calling). At times the conversation would actually escalate to the point where someone's Christianity would be called into question. The worst label of all would then be thrown onto the table... *heretic*.

I had to figure out what all the fuss was about. I had always just thought that when I was 14 years old, sitting in church listening to Rick Stanley preach, that *I* had decided that I wanted to get saved, to become a Christian. It was *my* choice, right? After all, I went down the aisle, I prayed, I shared my testimony with my friends, I got baptized, etc. I was the one pulling the trigger, right? Not so fast, I would soon find out.

I was told that the book I needed to read was by a man named R.C. Sproul called *Chosen By God*. If you are new to this whole debate on who "chose" who, then Sproul's book is truly an excellent primer on the Calvinistic side of the equation. Sproul is a reformed theologian and a godly man. I have since read numerous books of his and have been informed and inspired by his writings. I found this particular book at a local bookstore and devoured it in a matter of days. After reading the last page of Sproul's book, I had converted! I was now a five-point Calvinist.

I was able to join my fellow students in the student center and in late night dorm room discussions arguing the superiority of Calvinism over Arminianism. Oh, what is Arminianism? Arminianism is what I used to believe before reading Sproul's book, I just didn't know it!

John versus Jacob

John Calvin lived from 1509 to 1564 and is the father of what we today call Calvinism. Actually, in his day, there was no such-named doctrine. Calvin was a reformed theologian coming from the French protestant tradition. In Geneva, he would become influential over many refugees fleeing persecution. He is most famous for his *Institutes of Christian Religion.*

Jacob Arminius never knew John Calvin personally. He was born in the Netherlands in 1560, just four years before Calvin died. He too became a theological force after studying in Geneva. But Arminius took great exception to Calvin's teaching, especially in the area of God's election. His followers were devout, and after his death they gathered in 1610 to produce a document called the *Remonstrance.* In this document, they outlined the five points of Arminianism. Very briefly, here are those five points:

Free will. Man has the ability to freely choose to accept or reject God. It is his choice.

Conditional election. God chooses those for salvation who have first freely chosen Him.

Universal atonement. Jesus died for all of mankind. His blood is sufficient to cover the sins of all humanity.

Resistible grace. God, through the Holy Spirit, draws people to Himself, but Man has the freewill to resist and reject that drawing.

Perseverance of some saints. Some who come to Christ will persevere to the end while others will choose to reject God after salvation and will lose their salvation.

Of course, one good turn deserves another. So the followers of Calvin gathered to form a response to the *Remonstrance.* Gathering in 1618 at the Synod of Dort, this group of Calvin's disciples issued the *Canons of Dort*, which presented the five points of Calvinism. From these five points we have the famous TULIP. Each letter in the TULIP stands for one of Calvinism's five points.

Total depravity. Man is so utterly sinful and depraved that he does not have the ability, on his own, to choose God.

Unconditional election. Based on nothing an individual does, God, for His own reasons, chooses to elect some to salvation.

Limited atonement. Jesus died for the elect. His blood is sufficient to cover all the sins of those that God chooses for salvation.

Irresistible grace. Man's freewill is limited in that he is powerless to resist the drawing of God through the Holy Spirit.

Perseverance of all the saints. All those that God chose will remain faithful to the end. Once saved always saved.

I should point out that the debate is not as simplistic as I have presented it above. I have provided a very simple outline of the main points of contention. People in both camps argue the finer points of each of their own set of five points. For instance, I know some Arminians who believe that all the saints will persevere to the end, and I know some Calvinists that believe in unlimited atonement. This is where you will hear some say that they are three point or four point Calvinists. At this point the debate can become extremely muddled and at times confusing.

My experience has also been that public arguments over these points of doctrine really turn off lost people. A healthy dose of perspective is helpful when talking about these things. If you must argue with a fellow brother or sister about the points of this classic debate, do us all a favor, find a private place where you can duke it out and no one else has to witness the carnage.

Jeff versus Jeff

After engaging in the arena of debate for some time, I got tired of all the bickering myself. As time went on, my own five-point Calvinism gave way to a four-point version and then I later flirted with a three-point version. I found myself not being so certain. I felt this battle going on within myself over the truth. Romans 8 and 9 really resonated with me in terms of God's election and predestination. "He is the potter and I am the clay. I have no right to say to God what He will do with me." This was my thinking.

But other passages in the Bible dogged me. Especially in the book of Acts where we see the aggressive spread of the Gospel and so many people coming to salvation. There are numerous passages declaring that "whoever" calls on Jesus will be saved and find remission of sin (Acts 10:43, 11:14, 16:31). Even the book of Romans, which is heavy on God's election, and the Old Testament book of Joel seemed to be saying that anyone and everyone could have the chance to accept God if *they* choose to (Romans 10:13, Joel 2:32).

Now, I am not naïve. Theologians smarter than me on both sides can take what I have said along with the various biblical passages presented, and put their own interpretive slant on them. My point here is the struggle I have experienced between the two camps. I don't think I am alone. I approached a professor on campus when I was in college who "it was said" used to be a Calvinist. I asked him if this was true. He said it was. I asked him why he wasn't anymore and I will never forget his answer, "Because Calvinism always seems to explain everything about God and leave nothing to mystery. It is too neat. I am not sure I want a God that I can completely figure out." Hmmm… isn't that what we want, though? Full and complete answers to all our questions. Yet, it is true that when we get those answers, they can leave us unfulfilled. Sort of like the new toy you just had to have for Christmas when you were a kid, but two months later, is just gathering dust in your closet with all the other "must haves" of your past.

Over the years, I will admit that I have gravitated back and forth between the freewill and the election camps. I firmly believe that God chooses, and I firmly believe that I have freewill, that I get to choose. I am still not sure how that all goes together, but I know that I have been chosen.

Love

Let me tell you about a realization I had recently that has helped me tremendously to wrap my mind around this tension between "who chooses who." I have already shared within the pages of this book about how I met and fell in love with my wife, Julie. To this day I am in awe at the good fortune I had in finding someone as lovely, beautiful, and godly as my wife (but then again, maybe it was predestined!). Let me ask you this question:

Did Julie choose me or did I choose Julie?

The answer is obvious, isn't it? Yes! The answer is YES. She chose me *and* I chose her. And it all sort of happened simultaneously. You see that is the way love works. "For God so loved the world..." For I so love Julie...and she so loves me. And together we became three, then four and now five...and a dog! Can't you see how incredible this is? Love can never be programmed or coerced, or it isn't *love*. Love must be freely given and freely accepted for it to be the powerful force that it is. What makes Julie's love for me so intense is that I don't and can't make her love me. She has to choose this on her own. If she chooses to, she can refuse to love me tomorrow. That tension keeps our romance alive! Remember that movie *Love Potion Number 9*? It's about this guy who gets a love potion that makes girls love him. But it's all fake. In the end, he gets the girl he wants without the potion and yes, it makes all the difference in the world.

I recently read an article about the advances being made in artificial intelligence. The article made the claim that in the next 20-30 years, people will be having sexual relations with robots that look and act like real people. Can you imagine that? This was a serious article. But here's the problem. A robot, or a prostitute, might be able to satisfy a base and carnal desire, but neither will return love. The real world doesn't work like *Pretty Woman* or *Battlestar Galactica*.

Put simply, you can't program love. Since we are made in the Image of God, I think love works for God the same way it works for us. God is seeking love. Genuine, freely chosen love. "For God so loved..." and now He is looking for love in return. It seems to me that any love that has to be coerced through the flipping of a switch inside of us would be less satisfying than what God is seeking. Just like if I had to flip a switch in my wife (as if that were possible) in order to get her to love me. There would be something empty and artificial about that love. I have to *choose* to love God.

But it takes more than that, doesn't it? God has to choose me, too. What makes His love for me so special is that He didn't *have* to choose me. I don't necessarily think it works to say that God has generically chosen everybody and is sitting back waiting to see which individuals respond. There is something empty about that as well. When I chose Julie, she *had* to choose me too or else my choice was irrelevant. Did you ever have the hots for some girl (or guy) when you were a teenager, only to experience rejection? Or how special would it have been if your friends told you to ask a certain someone out, and that it was a "sure thing" because they would go out with anybody? Not that I have ever met anyone like that, but you get the point. The choosing *must* go both ways. It makes perfect sense when it comes to love and dating and marriage. And I think it makes sense when it comes to God.

Love Transforms

Let me bring this intermission to a close by declaring that love transforms. You are a sinner. You are lost, hungry and alone. The Image of God in you has been severely disfigured. But if you will choose God, if you will love Him, I can say with all confidence that God is waiting to choose and love you. Maybe He has already chosen you and is waiting. Read this next sentence carefully...

Love changes *everything*.

If you come to Christ, the *old* will pass away and everything will become *new*. You will become a new creation (2 Corinthians 5:17). God created you, and now He will re-create you. God is in the creation business. It is what He does best.

God gives us a very powerful promise when all the choosing is done. And here is the setup for Act 2.

> *And we all, with unveiled face, beholding the glory of the Lord, are being transformed into the same image from one degree of glory to another. For this comes from the Lord who is the Spirit.*

That's it. This passage from 2 Corinthians 3:18 nails it. No matter how ugly and distorted you think your life may be, the "good news" is that through Jesus Christ, God transforms. The Image of God in you can be restored. God takes you back to the body shop and bangs away on you to restore what was lost in the Garden. That is what the second half of this book is about. It is about *you*, being restored to what God intended for you to be all along, a special creation made in His image and likeness. This is where you get to join in the process, because it is a process. This is the best part of the book, the fun part, where we will look at five aspects of *you* as the restored Image of God.

ACT 2 – The Image of God

Restored

Chapter 6 – Saint

Aurelius Augustinus was a pagan. A sinner. Like so many young people, he ran from the religion of his parents. His mother, Monica, would plead with him to embrace her Christianity, but he would have none of it. Patricius, his father, was a pagan, and so "like father like son." Growing up in the beautiful seaside city of Carthage in Northern Africa, there was just too much going on to spend time on religion, too much fun to be had. And his father would show him the way. The Roman empire was not what it once was, but in the fourth century, it still provided a sense of security and safety, a sense of peace the world had never known before. So there just was no need to rely upon a deity. The emperor was all anyone needed.

Such peaceful times led to a lot of free time. Augustinus spent his free time thinking. He loved to think and ponder the great unanswered questions of the world. As youth gave way to maturity, it became obvious to young Augustinus that the world was not all well. People were still hungry, there were still wars and rumors of war, and the word on the street was that the empire was not doing well politically. Times were definitely changing, and that just led to more questions.

Augustinus found himself looking for answers in a direction that he once scoffed: religion. Unwilling to consider Christianity, he found himself attracted to the teachings of

Manichaeism.[1] Mani was from the ancient city of Babylon and his teachings reached worldwide prominence, stretching from China in the east to Rome in the west. Mani desperately wanted to be embraced as a Christian, and he even claimed he was a follower of Christ, but the church rejected him as a heretic. The reason was probably what drew a man like Augustinus to his teachings. Mani taught that salvation was found in knowledge, and that scratched the itch of Augustinus because he was all about knowledge and learning.[2]

As he continued to mature, Augustinus became a great rhetoretician. He was so good at what he did, that he landed a teaching position in his birth town of Tagaste. Being on the fast track to success, he would soon return to Carthage to teach at a school there. The trials of a teacher were a wake-up call. Augustinus became frustrated with his students who he viewed as unruly and wanting to only have fun. He decided he was wasting his time in Carthage, so he made the decision to move to Rome. He believed the best and brightest students resided in Rome, which made it the perfect place to start his own school. But kids will be kids, and Augustinus' frustrations grew with his new students as well. He was frustrated with his career and he was frustrated with his religion; Manichaeism, he was finding, was empty. He was also frustrated in his personal life. Running from the idea of marriage, he had acquired a concubine for some 15 years and together they had a son. Even this left him feeling empty.[3]

Augustinus' mother refused to give up on him. She pursued him to Milan and she, along with Ambrose, the bishop of Milan, began to greatly influence Augustinus' thinking. Or perhaps it was God, for I believe that Augustinus had been chosen, and because of this, he was ready to make a choice in his own life. Augustinus, at the age of 29, became a Christian. In his own testimony, he claims to have been walking through a garden in Milan when he heard a small child singing a song. The lyrics were simply, "take up and read." Convinced this message was for him, Augustinus found a copy of the Bible, and the first words he read were from Paul's letter to the Christians in Rome:

"Let us walk properly as in the daytime, not in orgies and drunkenness, not in sexual immorality and sensuality, not in quarreling and jealousy. But put on the Lord Jesus Christ, and make no provision for the flesh, to gratify its desires."[4]

This sealed the deal for Augustinus. He came to the understanding that he was a sinner and that he needed help. Help that could only come from Jesus Christ.

In one of his most famous writings called *Confessions*, Augustinus would later expand on this new realization of sin and his sinfulness.

"I still thought that it is not we who sin but some other nature that sins within us. It flattered my pride to think that I incurred no guilt and, when I did wrong, not to confess it... I preferred to excuse myself and blame this unknown thing which was in me but was not part of me. The truth, of course, was that it was all my own self, and my own impiety had divided me against myself. My sin was all the more incurable because I did not think myself a sinner".[5]

Over the course of the next ten years, Augustinus would go on to study for the priesthood and would later be named the Bishop of Hippo. Using his skill in rhetoric, he would become a prolific defender of the faith. He is considered today by many to be the most influential philosopher between Aristotle and Aquinas. His most famous writing is *The City of God*, wherein he defends Christianity against the charge that it was responsible for the eventual fall of the Roman

Empire.[6] Today Aurelius Augustinus is simply known as Saint Augustine.

The Path to Sainthood

From sinner to saint. That is Saint Augustine's story, and that is your story as well. What am I talking about, you say? Let me ask you this question: Have you ever met a saint? For some reason, when many people hear the word *saint*, they think of dead people. Select people who lived holy and godly lives are now viewed as *saints*. The idea of meeting a living, breathing saint is foreign to most people.

If you look up the word *saint* in a dictionary, you will get a definition similar to this, "one officially recognized especially through canonization or pre-eminent for holiness."[7] So who does the recognizing and canonizing? That would be the Roman Catholic Church. I would dare say that when most people consider who the saints are, they think of the various people canonized into sainthood by the Catholic Church. This is one of the reasons most of us think of saints as being dead people, because the Catholic Church does not bestow sainthood on someone until after they are dead. In fact, there are four criteria the Catholic Church uses to declare someone who is dead to be a saint.

First, the candidate cannot merely be dead, they must be dead for at least five years before being considered. I am not sure why five years, but I suspect that in the same way that "time heals old wounds," time gives us a perspective on the life of an individual. Are we still thinking and talking about this person years later, or have they simply dropped off the radar?

As a pastor, I have officiated many funerals, so I have been in the trenches of life and death. I have always found it interesting how quickly we move on when someone we know has died. Oh, I'm not talking about someone close like a father, child, or spouse; those deaths remain forever etched on our soul. I am talking about people outside our family. People we go to church with, someone in the community who is a fixture, or a celebrity that represents our generation. My experience is that when people like this die, they are very quickly forgotten. We move on, don't we? We are always focused on tomorrow rather than yesterday. It's more about who was at church today, or who was just elected mayor, or which star is the next Harrison Ford. I'm not saying that it's right, I'm just saying that it is. Time definitely does give us a perspective on the staying power of a dead person's life and influence.

The second quality of a saint is that they must have lived an exemplary life. Their reputation must be above reproach, and they are to have been a man or woman that was considered a true disciple of Christ in the highest sense. It is not as if the person doesn't have a past, though. Consider Saint Augustine. The man openly rejected and ran from Christ and his Church. He was sexually promiscuous. He had a child out of wedlock. I am sure there are a host of other skeletons in his closet we don't know about. But Augustine's life before Christ did not define him. What did define him was Jesus. If you were to put his life on a graph, you would see an upward trend. That's what you want to see in the life of a saint. An upward trend. Always growing and becoming more like Jesus.

Part of this process would be the examination of all the writings of the saintly candidate. The Church would be looking specifically for any heresy. This is not to say that everything the individual wrote had to be right, but there certainly would have to be agreement and support of the essentials of the faith in their writings.

I have often wondered what people would think if they looked at transcripts of all my sermons, all my blog entries, all my emails and letters, all the articles I've written, and even the words of this book. What would they think of me? You see, words are powerful and they do communicate the heart. What would people conclude about Jeff Crawford? I don't believe you would find heresy, but my prayer is that, put on a graph, you would see growth and maturity. Mostly, I hope you would see Jesus. And so the Church would dissect the words of a candidate for sainthood. Once the Church is satisfied with the "quality of life" requirement, the third component of sainthood could be considered.

The potential saint must next be beatified or blessed. For this to occur, the candidate must posthumously perform at least one miracle in response to a petition. If they have been martyred, however, they get a pass on this requirement and can move to the final step in being declared a saint. This third requirement can get pretty tricky since the person is dead. But miracles are considered proof that the candidate is indeed in heaven and is prepared to act as an interceder for those of us left on earth. What kind of miracle are we looking for? Well, it can be anything as long as the Catholic Church approves it.

Let's consider the case of Mother Teresa for instance. Born in 1910, Mother Teresa spent virtually her whole life working and ministering out of impoverished Calcutta. She dedicated her life "to the least of these." Her fame grew as she expanded her benevolent work around the globe, opening numerous Missionaries of Charity organizations. In 1979 she was awarded the Noble Peace Prize, and in the mid 1980s she even addressed the general assembly of the United Nations. At her death in 1997, there was virtually no one who did not know of Mother Teresa.

Because of her worldwide stature, there was tremendous pressure to move quickly through the process of declaring Mother Teresa a saint. In 1999, she was granted an exemption from the five-year, post-death waiting period. The examination of her life then began in earnest, with the

Diocesan Enquiry Team researching, interviewing witnesses to her life, and studying her writings. Their efforts produced 80 volumes of material, with each volume containing 450 pages.

The issue of the miracle came next. It was determined by the Diocesan Enquiry Team that Mother Teresa had indeed performed the miracle of curing a woman of a cancerous tumor in 1998.[8] With this requirement met, she achieved beatification on October 19, 2003. To date, Mother Teresa is just one step away from canonized sainthood. Considered "blessed," a candidate for sainthood can then be venerated by a region or group of people.

The final step in being declared a saint is the performance of one more miracles, even for martyrs. After this miracle is performed and verified by the church, the Pope will canonize the new saint and they will be recognized by the Church universal as a saint.[9] In the case of Mother Teresa, we are waiting for this final miracle in order to install upon her the title of Saint Teresa.

The Problem with the Path

There is a major problem with the path to sainthood as outlined by the Roman Catholic Church. It is not biblical. It is a manmade invention that, in my opinion, strips you and I of one of the most precious identities God has for us as the restored Image of God. Don't get me wrong, saints are very biblical. What I am saying is that the four step *path* to saint-hood is not.

To begin with, the whole idea of sainthood being some-thing that is bestowed on a person after death contradicts the overwhelming references to living saints in the Bible. In fact, the word saint occurs 87 times in the Bible with 64 of those occurrences being in the New Testament. The reason we see an explosion in the use of the term in the New Testament is that, with the advent of Jesus, everything changed.

We are told that once we choose God and He chooses us, we are "conformed to the image of his Son, in order that we might be the first born among many brothers."[10] Reflect for a moment on the significance of that verse. From sinners who are lost, hungry and alone, to something that is beginning to look like Jesus, the Son of God.

The image has changed.

The cocoon has split.

The caterpillar has emerged as a butterfly.

The power of God is on full display in people's lives, and we begin to see saints popping up all over the New Testament. That is why Paul closes his letter to the Philippians with this declaration of transformation,

> *Greet every saint in Christ Jesus. The brothers who are with me greet you. All the saints greet you, especially those of Caesar's household.*[11] *(emphasis mine)*

You see, saints aren't just dead, they are living and breathing and walking among us as well. In the above case, there were saints that weren't even Jews, God's chosen people. These saints were Gentiles. That means they were unclean and dirty pagans. The least of these. Some of them actually in the employ of the self-proclaimed deity of Caesar. Yet Paul calls these believers in Christ *saints*.

Saint Frank

Today I am performing the funeral for a saint. His name is Frank Shiflett. Frank was my Sunday School teacher when I was in fifth grade. When I came back to my home church to pastor it after being gone for almost 20 years, there was

Frank. He loved to tell people that everything I learned I got from him.

Frank died last week. He finally succumbed to an 18-year battle with cancer that reduced his lung capacity to 30% and ravaged his body. But here's the thing about Frank. He never, and I mean never, let it steal his life. He refused to be defined by his cancer and instead viewed it as part of his ministry.

Frank has two great kids. One son who is a pastor and a daughter who is married to a pastor. What a legacy. Frank lost his father when he was just 12, and I found out from talking to his kids that this was the reason he loved to teach children and invest his life into theirs in sort of a surrogate dad kind of role. He wanted to make sure kids had father figures who cared about them and to whom they could go.

I also learned from Frank's children and wife how real this man was. He was just a good ol' boy who spent his childhood days roaming around the secret places of eastern Oklahoma with his friends; sometime causing mischief like taking dynamite and blowing up outhouses (they'd check for occupancy first!). Frank loved to have fun and he always had a story to tell. And he lived his life to the end. In fact, he was snaking the plumbing on his house the day before his body finally gave out last week.

Frank also loved Jesus with a passion, and he loved his church. He was always there. No matter what. His doctor was worried about his balance, so he prescribed a walker. Frank would come to church *carrying* his folded-up walker. It made me laugh. When a brain tumor finally began to affect his hearing, he'd be at church with headphones on so he could hear me preach. Amazing.

As I was sharing memories with his family, the one word that came into my mind to describe Frank was saint. This man is and was a saint. He was a saint while he was walking and living among us. He was a saint as he died among us.

And this saint of earth is now a saint of heaven sitting beside the One who has finally healed him.

No five year waiting period.

No "writings" to examine.

No miracle to perform.

To be sure, he lived an exemplary life. Not a perfect life, but put on a graph, a life that always pointed up.

Frank Shiflett.

Saint Frank.

A Look in the Mirror

Let's go back to that question I asked several pages back. Have you ever met a saint? I hope your perspective has changed, for there are saints all around us. Not perfect people who have written lofty words and performed miracles. But imperfect people who have been captured by Jesus and are being transformed into his image. The Image of God restored.

Go look in a mirror. You will see a saint staring back at you. This may push you because you may not feel worthy. If you do feel worthy, that may indicate a problem! But as you look at yourself with all your warts and scars, physical and hidden, you know the ugly truth about yourself, so seeing a saint may be a hard thing to do. But it's true. Because of Jesus, you have journeyed from sinner to saint.

It is difficult to paint a picture where contrast is so stark. Love and hate. Good and evil. Black and white. Sinner and saint. But this just illustrates the power of Christ. Listen to me, to not see yourself as a saint is a slam on Jesus. You are saying he can't do it. You are too ugly to be made beautiful. Too weak to be made strong. Too defeated to be a conqueror. Too sinful to be saintly. Don't do that. You are talking about the God-Man who defeated death with life. He specializes in putting light in dark places. You are not outside his reach. He is in the saint-making business.

Blazing a New Path

When you see the word *saint* in the New Testament, what you are really looking at is the English translation of the Greek word *hag-ee-os*. While *hag-ee-os* is translated into the English word *saint* 64 times in the New Testament, it is also translated into another word 161 times. This other translation, the root meaning of *hag-ee-os*, is "holy". To be a saint is to be holy. Saints are the Holy Ones. Now you're probably really thinking you don't qualify for sainthood! You can't think that way. This is something God has done and is doing in you. A new path has been blazed. A path of holiness, and you are walking that path.

This is why the Christian feels guilty when he sins, whereas the non-Christian feels like sinning again. When you agree to walk the path of holiness, the Holy Spirit will slap you around when you get off the path. This is called discipline. Jesus declares that he disciplines those he loves.[12]

The non-Christian can sin without guilt because he does not belong to God. He is not on the path to holiness. He is walking a different path, a broad road, the Bible calls it. But it is a dangerous road that ends in total destruction. Most people travel this broad path, but a few find another path. A narrow path. A path of holiness that leads to eternal life. If that is the path you are walking my friend, then congratulations! You are one of the few of humanity to find it and walk it. It is a tough path because holiness does not come easily or naturally. But God will keep you in line and on track. Let's look a little closer at this new trail that has been blazed. The path of holiness. The path of the saint.

Death of the Old Man

The path to life begins with a death. Your death. Remember, you are a sinner. The penalty for sin is death. God is perfect and holy and He cannot let sin into heaven. So the sin and the sinner must die. This is the way it must be. This is why Jesus came and died. He was a trailblazer. He laid himself down as a sacrifice for your sin and for mine. He literally took upon himself the sin of all humanity. This is what Paul was talking about in Romans when he said,

> *"knowing this, that our old man was crucified with Him, that the body of sin might be done away with, that we should no longer be slaves of sin."*[13]

Crucifixion has only one end and that is death. Christ died on the cross and it was a real physical death. Paul wants us to *know* that, when we accept Christ into our lives, our former self dies. He calls this the old man. That's what sin does. It ages us prematurely. Have you ever met someone who has lived a *hard* life? A life of excess in every area? They look old, don't they? As they say at Lost Valley Ranch where Julie and I go each spring, they look like they've been "ridden hard and hung up wet."

I was reading a recent story about the British singing sensation Amy Winehouse. Winehouse lives a life of excess. At the age of 24, she is a compulsive cigarette smoker and a user of crack cocaine. The chronicles of her legal troubles, depression, and antics have made her infamous. Most recently, she was hospitalized and diagnosed with the early stages of emphysema. Can you imagine? Amy Winehouse's sin has aged her. She has the lungs of an old woman.

What happens to old, worn out people? They die. You see, sin really does lead to death. That death must occur in your life if you are going to walk the path of holiness. As

Paul explains, the body that is sinful must be done away with. You are a slave and you need to be freed. Isn't that interesting? Most people who don't want to be Christians say things like, "I don't want to have to live by a bunch of rules," or "I want to have fun and Jesus is just about a bunch of do's and don'ts," or even, "I want my freedom!" Yet it is not the Christian that is enslaved, it is the sinner. All the people in the world seeking to be free from the "tyranny" of Christianity have, in reality, enslaved themselves to sin voluntarily. Just ask a porn addict how hard it is to quit logging on. Or ask a smoker how hard it is to walk away from the rack of cigarettes at the gas station. Sin controls. Sin enslaves. But Jesus offers freedom…through death.

From Old to New

God specializes in creation and re-creation. When there is a death, what springs forth is new life. Jesus rose from the dead on the third day. When the old man dies, he is born again; *you* are born again. This is the power of the symbolism every time someone is baptized. The new convert stands in the water symbolic of old man. They are buried under the water just as Christ was buried in the tomb, then they are raised from the water just as Christ sprang forth from the depths of death. Every time I baptize someone, I even say that they "are raised to walk in a brand new life." Once again we turn to the words of Paul,

> *Therefore, if anyone is in Christ, he is a new creation; old things have passed away; behold, all things have become new.*[14]

When the Bible says "all things" here, it means *all* things. The Image of God restored. I am new and so are you. How this happens I simply don't know. It is God. It is what He

155

does. I am still me, understand. It's not that my personality has changed, or that I have become a robot void of uniqueness and originality. I have just been re-made to be what God intended for me to be all along. I am now a saint, a holy one walking the path of holiness. I have found the narrow path that leads to life, the path that few will ever find.

I think this is the part that most of us really struggle with. I think that the longer we are Christians, the more we may struggle because we simply don't feel new. The freshness of our conversion has passed, life is passing by, we make mistakes along the way, course corrections are made, etc. We know all our dirty little secrets and we just don't *feel* holy. But remember, you are on a path... a journey of sorts.

Calvin Miller has said it best when he explains that, "Saints do not spring holy or whole from the forehead of God. They are made, crisis by crisis, need by need. Those who wish to be conformed to his image only make real progress after they discover their own insufficiency."[15] What Miller is saying is that holiness is a *process*.

We have a theological word for this called *sanctification*. Sanctification means to be set apart, to be different. It implies that this is a journey. On this journey God has His part and you have your part. God's part is to equip you with everything you will need for the journey. His part is to also test you to see if you're serious about this path of holiness. Some people stumble upon this path but aren't serious, and eventually they go back to the big, wide road where they can sin and feel no guilt. They'd rather be a slave than be free. Why do they think this way? Because for them, the old man never died.

Our churches are full of people like this, people trying to fake it. Trying to make themselves look like they are walking the saintly path when they are really walking their own path. They can fake it for a while, but in time, all will be revealed. So God tests. He puts us in crises and situations designed to see if we have really killed the old man. This is why Paul emphasized again when he was writing to the church at Ephesus to,

> *"put off, concerning your former conduct, the old man which grows corrupt according to the deceitful lusts, and be renewed in the spirit of your mind, and that you put on the new man which was created according to God, in true righteousness and holiness."*[16]

Even though the old man is dead, he is attempting a resurrection of his own. He must be continually beat down. Jesus emphasizes that we must take up our cross *daily* and follow him.[17] I said it once, but it bears repeating. You are on a journey and the journey will separate those who have truly died to self and those who are pretending. Paul repeats this same message to the church at Colossae,

> *"But now you yourselves are to put off all these: anger, wrath, malice, blasphemy, filthy language out of your mouth. Do not lie to one another, since you have put off the old man with his deeds, and have put on the new man who is renewed in knowledge according to the image of Him who created him* [emphasis mine]*."*[18]

There you have it. The old man is killed, the new man rises, and the Image of God is restored. The path of holiness begins and you are called a saint.

From Far to Near

We all walk a path. It is a part of life. There are those who believe that all paths lead to God, but this is incorrect. Oh, there are many paths to be sure, but all of them, except for one, have the same thing in common. They all lead *away* from God. It may seem odd that a path that claims to lead people *to* God actually leads them *away* from God, but it is true. If you follow the path of Allah, you will in reality be walking away from God. If you follow the path paved by Joseph Smith and the Mormon Church, you will be walking away from God, even though they are certain that you are walking toward Him. If you follow the path of Hinduism, you are walking away from God. If you follow the New Age path that claims that you are your own God, you are most certainly walking away from the one and only true God.

Buddhism has what it calls the *Eight-fold Path*. Buddhism overtly rejects the idea of God and focuses instead on the individual's search for what it calls Nirvana. Nirvana most literally means "blow out." This belief system teaches that through an endless process of reincarnation, you get chance after chance to get it right. Getting it right means to walk the *Eight-fold Path* which, when done properly, will lead you to Nirvana and stop the progression of reincarnation. This path is as follows:

1. **Right Belief** – understanding the Four Noble Truths
2. **Right Resolve** – maintaining pure motives
3. **Right Speech** – speaking truthfully
4. **Right Conduct** – living peacefully and honestly
5. **Right Livelihood** – choosing a job that harms no one
6. **Right Effect** – seeking knowledge with self-control
7. **Right Thought** – keeping an active, self-critical mind
8. **Right Concentration** – practicing meditation and yoga with zeal

It all sounds great on the surface and many people follow this path. But this path and all the paths mentioned above lead in the same direction, and that is away from God. Only by killing the old man and being reborn in Jesus Christ can you begin to walk a new path. A path where something remarkable occurs. Paul put it this way,

> *"But now in Christ Jesus you who once were far off have been brought near by the blood of Christ."*[19]

Adam and Eve walked away from God when they chose the path of self in the Garden of Eden. Mankind has been walking away from God ever since. The path of holiness is a path whereby we return to Eden. We who were once far away from God are brought near. From sinner to saint. Fellowship with God is restored. Fellowship with one another is restored. The Image of God is restored.

Chapter 7 – Creator

"In the beginning God created…." When we are first introduced to God in the Bible, we see Him doing what he does best – creating. When the biblical epic concludes in the book of Revelation, we see God re-creating. The whole idea of creation is a mega-theme of the Bible.

God is first and foremost a Creator. He loves to make things. There seems to be no end to the *creative* nature of God. As I said in an earlier chapter, I love the mountains of Colorado. They serve as an annual retreat from the manmade creation of the city. I love the smell of the evergreen trees. I love the indescribable sound of the wind blowing through the valley and passing through those same trees. It is almost as if God is whispering to me.

There is one particular hike that Julie and I discovered a few years ago along a nature path of sorts. It's not really a hike as much as it is a walk. It is a stunning path that starts on a low ridge and drops down into a heavily wooded area. Before long you are hemmed in by the landscape, and then suddenly the trail springs open into an aspen meadow. As you continue, you pass the base of a mountain where massive granite rocks have fallen and piled up likes a child's building blocks. The path descends and follows a babbling brook that eventually becomes a stream and then a fast flowing river.

Last year as Julie and I walked this path, it began to snow. Not a heavy snow, but the very gentle kind with virtually no wind. Huge snow flakes fell all around us as we walked. Have you ever noticed how nature becomes very quiet when it snows? That is exactly what we heard as we walked, no sound at all. Pure peace and quiet in the midst of a stunning landscape being draped with the soft cotton fabric of heaven. Julie and I were in awe. It was truly unforgettable.

And God created all of it.

Six Days

You can learn about someone by observing what they create. In the same way, you can learn about God by looking at His creation. It never fails that every time I make my pilgrimage to the mountains, I learn new things about God. I know that God loves variety. Even though our destination in the mountains is the same each year, our experience is always different. I know that God loves color. Every shade of the rainbow is present between the sky and the earth. I know that God loves life, for the mountains are teeming with life. Life in the air, life roaming the earth, life in the water, and life within the dirt of the earth itself. I know that God loves texture and temperature and smell, and I could go on and on. All of this and more is present in God's creation. Here's the mind blowing thing about it: He created it all in six days!

I realize that there is a debate these days about the length of the creation event, even among Christians. Did God really create the heavens and the earth in six literal days? Or was it in six longer lengths of time? Or is the creation account in Genesis just a metaphor, and did evolutionary processes give us creation over the course of millions of years? Let me tell you what I believe. I believe that God did it all in six days. Period.

I know all the arguments about evolutionary theory. I have studied them in depth, and do you know what they are? They are just what I said, *theory*. It takes as much, if not more, faith to believe evolutionary theory as it does to believe creation. The holes in evolutionary theory are stunning. I am ever amazed at those who shoot arrows at Christians for being mindless, but refuse to look at the deficits in their own ways of thinking.

Yes, I know that the sun and moon were not created until the fourth day, so how could there be literal 24 hour days before then, on those "days" that God created land and water and vegetables and trees? But here is why I believe in a literal six day creation, and it's a two-fold answer. Part one, I wasn't there and so I have to accept by faith the word of someone who was. The *only* one who was there was God. And He said six days. Part two, to believe anything else means I have to disprove what is literally said in the biblical text itself, and I simply do not have enough information inside or outside the Bible to do that. Any other explanation is a faith step away from the written testimony of God.

Let me say one more thing about the creation event that is much more important than the length of time that God spent doing it. I think we can get so caught up in arguing about these things that we miss the point, and I am not sure that the point of Genesis 1 is to give us a cookbook on how God did it anyway. I think the point is less about *creation* and more about God, the *Creator*. So regardless of what you personally believe about how long God took to create things, let me ask you this question:

Do you believe *God can create the heavens and the earth in six days?*

You see, I believe that God did it all in six days. I also believe that He *could have* done it in six minutes. Or for that matter six seconds if He had wanted to! The point, my friend, is not what you believe about creation, but what you believe about the God who creates. Is your God big enough that He can snap His fingers and the world can fall into place?

The Crowning Act of Creation

"So God created man in his own image, in the image of God he created him; male and female he created them (Genesis 1:27)." The crowning act of creation was Man. The word *created* is used three times in this one verse. God wants us to know that life comes from Him. This is important for us to understand for several reasons.

Creation of Life is God's Business

The original deception was when the snake told Eve that she could be like God. Mankind has been striving ever since to *be* god. The ultimate expression of godhood is the ability to create life. Never before in our history has mankind been tinkering with the building blocks of life more than what we are today.

Consider cloning. The whole idea is that you no longer need a male and a female to reproduce. All you need is a woman's egg that is stripped of its DNA. Then you take the DNA of someone and insert it into the egg, you implant the egg in a womb, and nine months later, you have an exact physical replica of the original DNA donor. This has not yet been tried with humans (that we know of), but the cloning procedure has been used successfully with animals. I would put an asterisk beside the word successful and note that Dolly the sheep was cloned only after numerous failed attempts resulting in horrific deformations.

We all know that it is just a matter of time before someone, somewhere will attempt to clone a human. This means that two lesbians can have their "own" child. No more need for a man, or for sexual reproduction. It can all be done in a lab. Man can create. Man can be a god.

The human genome project is a marvel of man's mind and a symbol of his step toward godhood. Now that the human DNA has been mapped, scientists are isolating the specific genes that relate to every aspect of who we are from hair color, to height, to eye color, etc. The original idea behind the human genome project was to identify the specific genes that cause diseases such as diabetes, breast cancer, etc. It is hoped that by isolating these genes, they can be removed from embryos, and then children can be born without a future that contains these diseases. It all sounds like paradise, doesn't it? It is playing tinker-toys with the building blocks of life on the largest scale possible.

We are perhaps a generation or less away from the point at which a couple, ready to have children, will not go see an OB/GYN first, but instead their local geneticist. They will sit down with this qualified professional who will pull up a slide of the 20 plus embryos that the couple have "created". The geneticist will inform the couple which embryos will grow into children with brown hair, or perhaps even red hair! He will describe their eye color and their height. He will tell them which embryos have a genetic disposition for a higher IQ, and will thus do better in school, score higher on the ACT, and land that scholarship for college — making mom and dad proud, of course. Most importantly, he will tell the young couple which embryos are predisposed to heart disease and alcoholism. Which ones have a likelihood of ADHD and dyslexia. He will then discuss genetic alteration options with the couple.

Designer children is what we are talking about. Taking God completely out of the mix. Sound like science fiction? Science for sure, but no longer fiction. The technology and know-how is already here. This is the future of childbirth.

The challenge for the church is to help advise and guide young couples as the intense pressure to play god descends upon them. It will feel very natural and be marketed as such. I mean, what kind of loving parent would not want to give their kid the best start in life? Parents who leave childbirth up to chance, conceiving the "old fashioned way" by having sexual relations, could be demonized as foolish, uncaring, and fanatically religious. The church had better get ready because the future is now.

Termination of Life is God's Business

Life is a serious thing to God. When Cain committed the first murder in the Bible, God marked him for life so that all would know what he had done. God wanted everyone to know that the taking of a human life is the most serious of sins. Man does not create life and it is not his place to terminate life.

In Genesis 9, God re-created the earth in a manner of speaking. Three chapters earlier, we saw God fed up with all the sin that dominated the earth, so He decided to start over. He sent a great flood that terminated all human life except for the family of Noah. When God was ready to re-boot creation, he instructed Noah,

> *Whoever sheds the blood of man, by man shall his blood be shed, for God made man in his own image.*[1]

God advocates capital punishment for the sin of murder. Why? Because God declares that when a person attacks and kills another human being, what they have really done is attack the Image of God. God takes it very personally. It's as if He feels attacked Himself. And God will simply not tolerate this. Think about that the next time you get mad at someone and have harmful thoughts toward them!

Let's put this in a modern context. The Center for Bio-Ethical Reform reports that in the United States alone, approximately 1.36 million abortions occur each year, averaging out to around 3,700 every day. On a worldwide scale, there are 46 million abortions performed each year. That's 126,000 babies killed in the womb every day.[2]

The biggest defense to these killings is that what is being "extracted" from the woman's body is not a baby but is "tissue." Any honest examination of the "tissue" being extracted will inform the viewer it is something much more than tissue. Arms, legs, a head, fingers, and toes are much more than tissue. They are, in fact, arms, legs, a head, fingers, and toes!

Years ago when I would teach worldview philosophy to high school seniors, the curriculum I used had a unit on abortion. This curriculum had a most helpful tool to understanding the differences between the born and the unborn. I offer it here for your consideration. It is presented in the form of an acronym: **SLED**.[3]

Size – The difference between the born and the unborn is size. A fetus is smaller than a newborn. But does that make him/her less human? My 11-year-old daughter is smaller than me, but she is just as much a person as I am.

Level of Development – The unborn are not as developed as the born. Once again, my daughter is not as developed as I am. Her brain is still developing and her ability to think abstractly is still in process. On a physical level, she is not yet as developed as her mother. She has yet to enter puberty. But is she less a person than her mother? Certainly not!

Environment – The environment of the womb is far different than the environment that the born live in. But once again, what does that have to do with personhood? When I get in a plane and fly 20,000 feet in the air, my environment has changed, but I am still me. If I don a wetsuit and an air tank and go diving, I may be in a different environment, but I am still a human being.

Dependency – This is important because many advocates to abortion note than the fetus cannot survive apart from the mother. The unborn are dependent. But as the born move through life, we also develop dependencies. My aunt was on oxygen before she passed away. Everywhere she went, she had that tank with her. She also had diabetes and had to spend hours each week in the hospital hooked up to a dialysis machine. Was she not a person anymore because she was dependent on these things?

I would propose that the above four differences are the only differences between the born and the unborn. The question is this, do any of these four differences justify the unborn as not human? No way. The unborn are people just like you and me. Once they are conceived, all they need are nourishment and time to grow bigger. That makes them no different than those living outside the womb. To terminate their lives would be murder, just like if someone were to kill you. It is an attack on the Image of God. God and God alone determines when a life He created will end.

In the Image of the Creator

God gives and God takes away. He creates and He destroys. You and I are created in His image and likeness. That means that at our core, we are made to be creators as well. Have you ever noticed that there is something about humanity that leads us to never being content with the world the way it is? Mankind is always seeking to shape this planet we live on. To learn and to grow and to expand and to make life better.

Thomas Edison created the light bulb. Henry Ford created the Model T. Bill Gates created Windows. Steve Jobs created the iPod. These men all had one thing in common. They were not satisfied, so they created. As a result, life is better. This is the way God intended it to be. God gave us the world to rule. It is our laboratory whereby we can experiment. God said that this planet is ours and that we are to go and to subdue it and to have dominion over it. That is what we do when we create.

But there is a problem. The Image of God becomes corrupted, and so while we are still creators, the things we create tend to lead us away from God instead of toward Him. Man has become the master of using his creative gifts to corrupt self and others. When Paul was writing to the church in Rome, he echoed this sentiment by describing those who have rejected God as "inventors of evil."[4] As if there are not enough ways to reject and rebel against God already, human beings are experts at finding and creating new ways.

Take the internet as an example. The creation of the internet in and of itself is not a bad thing. It is a demonstration of our creative ability as a people to connect and share information without being limited by geography. But because Man is so good at creating new ways to be evil, the internet has become the leading source of pornography distribution in the world. What once was limited to adult bookstores in shady parts of town is now accessible in every home in the world with just the click of a mouse. Further, pornography itself is an example of taking God's creation, the human body, which is lovely and beautiful, and exploiting it to the point of worship. When someone views pornography, what they are really doing is worshiping creation rather than the Creator.

God has redeemed all those who turn to His Son Jesus Christ. The Image of God is restored. I firmly believe that it is our mandate as Christians to be creators of good. Look at what Paul said to the church at Philippi,

> *"Finally, brothers, whatever is true, whatever is honorable, whatever is just, whatever is pure, whatever is lovely, whatever is commendable, if there is any excellence, if there is anything worthy of praise, think about these things."*[5]

I would contend that the above list should be the focus of our creative efforts as Christians. We should be creating things that are lovely and pure. Things that are honorable and excellent. Our creative efforts ought to lead to the praise and worship of our Creator. In doing so, we can fulfill God's command to subdue the earth and the evil that is within it.

Creative Cramps

As children, we are creative geniuses. All kids are. What kid doesn't constantly create with the raw tools of his or her world? My son Grayson is six years old and he is always making something. I have a picture in my Bible of a monster that Grayson drew for me. He put it in there himself because he wanted me to have a bookmark. I really don't have any practical use for it, but I can't bring myself to remove it because my son created it for me. He created it for me because he loves me and he wants me to have a picture of a monster in my Bible so that when I see it I will think of him.

Grayson makes all kinds of other things, too. Things with Play-Doh and clay. Things with paper, scissors and crayons.

Things with Legos and K'Nex. He just loves to create and make things. Every time he makes something, he wants to show it off. He wants people to see. I think that is part of our creative make-up as well. The need to create so that people can affirm us.

We all know what happens as we grow older, don't we? We eventually put the scissors and glue away. The Legos are stored in the back of the closet. We "outgrow" these childish activities. The problem is that while we may outgrow the mode of our creativity, we should never outgrow the activity of creating. Yet too many times we do. My two older children (ages 14 and 12) are not nearly as creative as they used to be when they were Grayson's age. For that matter, I am not nearly as creative as they are. I have allowed "maturity" to knock the creative juices out of me. It is sad and it is not what God desires for us.

Ed Young, in his book on creative leadership, calls this creative cramps. Ed writes,

> "Most people have trouble realizing their creative potential, because at some point along life's journey their creativity was beaten out of them. Most of us suffer from a creative cramp somewhere during the course of our lives."[6]

In addition, studies show that children age six and under score remarkably high, in the ninetieth percentile, in their creative ability. But by age seven there begins a sharp decline, a creative cramp.[7] This creative cramping can last and expand into adulthood, almost completely choking out the creative process in many people.

I was able to witness a recovery of creativity in my children this summer. Sort of. We went to South Padre Island for our family vacation to spend a week on the beach. It was the first time we had ever done anything like this as a family and it was great. The weather was perfect and the waters of the gulf were invigorating. Then there was the sand. South Padre Island is basically a two-and-a-half mile development on a barrier island with picture perfect sand. Let me tell you that there is nothing like a beach full of sand to get the creative juices going.

My kids, all of them, loved the sand. Grayson and Madison built sand castle after sand castle. Garrett attempted to dig the deepest hole he could. I was amazed that they could sit there for hours, day after day, and never get bored of playing in the sand. The beach is a canvas of sorts, and it just screams with potential. My children were determined to see how far that potential could go. The unique thing about the beach is that each night, the tide wipes the canvas clean so that you can start anew the next day.

Creative Recovery

I think that most of us need the kind of creative recovery that the tide of the ocean brings. We need the canvas wiped clean. We need to see the world in a new and fresh way. We need to be able to see *our* footprints in the sand and know that we are making a difference. Too many of us have bought into the lie that we need to "grow up" and get serious about life. I say that nothing could be more serious than the act of creating.

There is an aspect of having children that I have never gotten over. It is the overwhelming feeling that I shared in the creative process of a human life. When I look at my kids, I see aspects of me in them. Hair texture, eye color, skin tone. My wife and I came together in an act of love and through God's sovereignty, we created. The fact that God allows us to share in the creation of life (an act that He is ultimately responsible for) is simply amazing. That is why parents are so proud of their kids. It is why we hurt so badly when we see them going in the wrong direction.

This is just one example of our nature as creations of God to be creators ourselves. I believe Christians should be the most creative people on the planet.

Let me challenge you in this way...

Go ye therefore and create.

How?

Well, to begin with, what do you *love* to do? Not what do you do for a living, but what do you love to do? The two are not always the same. My wife, Julie, loves two things, the first being scrapbooking. She creates the most amazing scrapbooks that chronicle our life together as a family. It is an ever-growing project as the years pass by. Several years ago, she had the idea to create scrapbooks just for the kids that chronicle their own lives. She plans to give those books to each of our children when they marry one day. Pretty cool, huh?

My wife also loves to cook. In recent years, she has become health conscious and she loves to find ways to cook healthy food that tastes really good. Let me say that she is awesome at this. I have never eaten more broccoli, squash, peppers, and zucchini in my life and loved it! She is an amazing creator of fine cuisine.

What do I love to do? I love to read and to think. My bachelor's degree was in philosophy (don't laugh), so I love to read and to learn. I am always thinking about what I would say. I guess you could say that this book that you are reading is my creative contribution to the world based on what I love. Another thing I love to do is teach and preach God's Word. Taking that passion, I try to constantly push myself to find new and creative ways to teach and preach. I will use video, stories, whatever. I get great joy in dissecting the text and finding a new angle for sharing the Ancient Words in today's world.

The business administrator of our church is a guy named Don Lehman. Don is an amazing man. He came to us from a job in Human Resources at a major media company. Don is a great business administrator. But what Don loves to do is build things with his hands. As a result, he has taken what he loves and has made himself even more valuable to our church. On many days you can come to our church and see Don in work jeans, covered in sheet rock dust. His office is well equipped with power tools. He is a machine. I could tell him that he needs to put all the 2x4's away and concentrate on his desk job, but if I did that I'd be taking him away from what he loves, and as a result, he probably wouldn't be as good of a business administrator!

What about you? What do you love to do? Do you love building things like Don? Do you love music? Can you play an instrument? Do you love to write? To paint? Can you sing? Don't let yourself be limited by traditional ways of thinking. Remember we have to be *creative*.

Let me tell you about Danny Hill. Danny is one of the coolest men in my church. He's got a wonderful wife and two great teenage kids. Danny is a successful business man owning his own company which operates locally. But what Danny really loves to do is ride motorcycles. He has figured out a way to creatively merge his love for motorcycles with his faith. He is a member of the local chapter of bike organization called Bikers Against Child Abuse (BACA). Danny rides with BACA and uses it as an opportunity to tell people about Jesus.

Danny has also made the investment to put his faith on his custom Bonneville by way of a special paint scheme. It is a stylized crucifix with flames inside of its structure with the words "Where will you spend eternity?" across its top. The biblical passages of Romans 5:8 and Romans 10:9 are at the bottom. In Danny's words, "This was done as to be a witnessing 'billboard' to passers-by at bike rallies and to give the timid a clue as to where in the Bible to find a passage on salvation."

When Danny parks his bike, he leaves several "biker Bibles" on the seat. A couple of years ago, Danny gave me a copy of one of these New Testaments which has the title, *Hope for the Highway,* on it.

When our church wanted to create a special event for fathers on Father's Day, a car and bike show, I turned to Danny to get the word out among the biking community. As a result, bikers showed up at church on Father's Day. It was pretty cool.

I'll ask it again, what do you love to do? Whatever it is, and I mean *whatever* it is, I want to challenge you to take that passion and creatively direct it for use in God's Kingdom.

The Tyranny of Technology

We live today under what I call the "tyranny of technology." Do you remember when they said that computers would make our lives easier? We would be able to do our work so much faster and more efficiently, and as a result, we would have more time left over to relax and enjoy life. I'm in! How about you?

That's not the way it ended up working, is it? What happened was that computers did indeed help us get our work done quicker and more efficiently, but then we took the left-over time and decided that we could use it to do *more* work. In fact, we began to feel *compelled* to do more work. Time is money and the more we can produce the more we can make. Right? When it seems that everyone else is producing more, we feel compelled to keep up. What started out as a great piece of technology designed to make our lives easier has become a piece of technology that has created more for us to do than ever before. The tyranny of technology.

Take cell phones as another example. It was supposed to work the same way. I can talk to anyone anywhere and get stuff done more quickly. But it just doesn't work that way. Let me tell you that I hate my cell phone. Instead of it being my link to the world, it has become the world's link to me. No matter where I am, people have access to me. If I decide to not answer a call, people get mad because they know I have a cell phone and they know that I know they're calling. When I go on vacation I have to literally turn my cell phone off.

If there is one thing I hate more than cell phones, it is email. I HATE email. Email is a great invention, once again, designed to make our lives easier and more productive. But what email turns into, more times than not, is everyone else's "to-do" list for me. Email is great for the distribution of information, but it is terrible for just about everything else. Email has given us an "out" for personal voice-to-voice or face-to-face communication. I can't even count the number of times email has caused a problem that never would have been if two people had just sat down and talked. Email has no tone, or voice, or life to it. It is just words that can easily be misunderstood. The main reason I hate email is that it keeps me from doing the things I really need to be doing as a pastor.

My point is that the world is moving faster and faster all the time. Technology was supposed to be our great deliverer from busy-ness, but it has just made us busier. We live in a 24/7 world today. The days of 9-5 are gone. We work all the time. When we are sleeping, the Japanese Nikkei Index is rolling along, impacting the lives of investors before they even crawl out of bed on this side of the globe. It's just crazy and it will only get crazier.

The words of one caller to a radio talk show are telling, "I feel like my problem with time is that I have gotten into a bad habit of filling every minute of my time with something

I think absolutely must be done, and now I will not allow myself down time without feeling like I should be doing something. I am always exhausted from overworking myself that I am cranky and stressed out and I am not much fun to be with."[8] Sound like anyone you know?

Holy Resting

I think it is very interesting that when God was done creating, the Bible points out what He did next,

"Thus the heavens and the earth were finished, and all the host of them. And on the seventh day God finished his work that he had done, and he rested on the seventh day from all his work that he had done. So God blessed the seventh day and made it holy, because on it God rested from all his work that he had done in creation."[9]

Did God really need to rest? I don't think so. I think what God was doing was giving you and me a powerful message about the importance of *Sabbath*. Jews pronounce the word *Sha-bawth*. What God is telling us is that it is okay to rest. In fact, it is more than just okay, it is *commanded*. We see this echoed in the fourth of the ten commandments in the book of Exodus,

"Remember the Sabbath day, to keep it holy. Six days you shall labor, and do all your work, but the seventh day is a Sabbath to the LORD your God. On it you shall not do any work, you, or your son, or your daughter, your male servant, or your female servant, or your livestock, or the sojourner who is within your gates. For in six days the LORD made heaven and earth, the sea, and all that is in them, and rested the

seventh day. Therefore the LORD *blessed the Sabbath day and made it holy."* [10]

We are really good as Christians about staying busy. Our churches are over-programmed and many of our people are just worked to death in the service of God. Work is good and it is good to be busy about the business of the Kingdom, but we must also rest. We are not fully spirit; we also have a body of flesh and bones that needs to rest. God actually calls this act of resting *holy*.

Rabbi Joseph Telushkin reminds us that to a Jew, the *Sha-bawth* is really a holiday. [11] This only makes sense because both of the above passages call *Sha-bawth* a "holy-day," which is where we get the word *holiday* from in the first place.

This idea of Sunday being a "holiday" is interesting, because when most people today think of "going to church," they get turned off. They'd rather sleep in, watch football, or go to the lake. We don't think of Sundays as a holiday. When I think of a holiday, I think of Christmas, and family, and friends, and warm feelings, and great food, and the exchange of gifts. To me that is a holiday. But the Bible tells us that the *Sha-bawth* is God's holiday for us. This stretches our thinking. Sundays should be so much more than we make them. More than just a day to get up and go to church and put a check in the box. "Okay, I've done the church thing, now I can get on with what I really want to do today," tends to be our thinking.

What to Do and What Not to Do...That Is the Question

What kind of things should we be doing on *Sha-bawth*? First of all, let me say that I don't think there is anything magical about Sunday as a day. In fact, Sunday is technically not the seventh day of the week, it is the first day of the week. This is why Jews celebrate *Sha-bawth* beginning at sunset on Friday until sunset on Saturday. If we are going to get picky about things, Friday into Saturday is the seventh day of the week. Christians have made it a practice to celebrate what we call the Sabbath on Sundays because that is the day Jesus rose from the grave. Still you have some Christians, such as Seventh Day Adventists, who take the command to keep the *Sha-bawth* very literally and they worship on Saturdays.

I personally don't think that the actual day is the point God was trying to make. *Sha-Bawth*, I believe, is less about a particular day and more about a particular practice, the practice of *holy resting*. What does that mean? Consider these Jewish minimal standards to be observed on *Sha-bawth*[12]:

1. No working for wages or competing for awards.
2. Making some time to relax and do nothing.
3. Reading and studying religious materials.
4. Playing with children, spouse and family.
5. Taking leisurely strolls.
6. Enjoying wonderful meals and discussions with friends and neighbors.
7. Talking with children about their everyday lives, thoughts, and feelings.
8. Attending religious services, lectures and discussions.
9. Praying and contemplating.
10. Lovemaking with your spouse (reconnecting in mind, body, and spirit).

I love this list. It sounds much more like the description of a holiday than the Sunday ritual that I grew up with. Is church attendance and worship a part of *Sha-bawth*? Absolutely! But there is so much more that God has for us. Don't you see? *Sha-Bawth* is like God's weekly holiday for us. Can you imagine a group of employees going into the office on a holiday such as Memorial Day and saying, "Thanks for the holiday but no thanks, I'd rather work." That's crazy.

What is also crazy is that there are people who work seven days a week and never celebrate *Sha-bawth*. And there are people who think *Sha-bawth* is only about themselves and their desires. And there are people who think that if they show up at church from 11:00 – 12:00, they have "celebrated" *Sha-bawth*. And there are also people who think that if they show up at church at 8:30 in the morning and stay all afternoon attending meetings and working, and then attend one more worship service at 6:30 and get home utterly exhausted, they have celebrated *Sha-bawth*. I would say that all of these have missed the point of *Sha-Bawth* to one degree or another.

The Key

I became convicted about a year ago that we were just wearing our people out on Sundays. We have a really packed schedule in the mornings starting for some of our folks at 7:00 am, and not concluding until after noon. We were also in a habit of scheduling all our "special" meetings in the afternoons. Our Board of Overseers and our Deacons have always reserved Sunday afternoons for meetings and conducting church business. I had the distinct sense that when these godly men showed up to meet and serve, it wasn't necessarily the easiest thing for them. They had gone home from a long morning, eaten and cleaned up lunch, sat down for just a few minutes (and we all know what happens when you sit down on Sunday afternoons), and then they had to get back up to come to a meeting. To make matters a little more difficult, we have Sunday evening services during the school year, which meant these men had to then turn around and run home to get their families and return to church.

We were effectively taking guys away from their families, working them, and then running them around town to gather their families back up. Hardly what you could call a day of rest and certainly not in the spirit of *Sha-bawth*.

We made the decision among our various groups to no longer have meetings to conduct business on Sundays. We can do that during the week. Sundays really should be reserved. If we are going to be serious about *Sha-bawth*, we do not need to view Sundays as the best time for people to work.

The key to *Sha-bawth* is what I will call *sacred time*. Sacred time is time spent doing all the things that you simply do not have time to do the other six days while you are under the tyranny of technology. It means you should turn off your cell phone and refuse to check your email. It means you should worship God with your family and with a community of like-minded believers. It means you should eat really good food with friends. It means you should take an afternoon nap. It means you should weed your garden IF that is something you love and not loathe. It means you should make love to your spouse and re-connect with them in body and spirit. It means you should teach your son to play chess. It means you should learn to play X-Box and let your son teach you. It means you should read about God and study His Word and seek to grow deeper. It means you should model all of these and other *sacred time* practices to your children so that they can grow up and model them for your grandkids one day. I know, it sounds like a lot to cram into just one day. But don't worry! As we preachers say, "Sunday's on the way!" God will give you *another* holy-day, a holiday, in just seven more days. What a gift!

Re-Creation

In the beginning God created. And then after six days, God re-created. The word *recreation* is really just the word *re-creation* without the hyphen. In the past, Christians have not been very good at seeing the value of recreation. I know too many Christians who are very serious, all the time. They don't know how to have fun, how to relax. They don't understand the critical importance of recreation. They just don't see it as the holy activity that it is. But God is clear. *Sha-bawth* is woven into the very fabric of creation itself. God feels so strongly about the human need for re-creation that he included it in His personal list of ten laws. Sadly, it doesn't make the top ten list of the most important Christian disciplines of most believers I know.

The point of this chapter is simple. Go ye therefore as the restored Image of God and be creators. Work and toil for six days and exploit the things you love to do in order to create a better world for those around you. Then step back, and take a day. Just one day out of seven, and let God *re-create* something special in you.

Chapter 8 – Forgiver

Our Father in heaven, hallowed be your name. Your kingdom come, your will be done, on earth as it is in heaven. Give us this day our daily bread, and forgive us our debts, as we also have forgiven our debtors....[1]

This is how Jesus told us to pray. But it is more than a prayer, isn't it? This prayer also reflects who we are as the restored Image of God. Christians are to be a forgiving people because God is a forgiving God. This is what it means to be the Image of God, to be in His likeness. But I think many, many Christians struggle with forgiveness.

Getting Over It

At times we struggle with the receiving end of forgiveness. I know I do. There are those times that I am so disgusted at myself and the way that I am (it's that old man thing coming back), that I just can't see how God could love me and forgive me. But He does. He really does. It is now my job to *get over it*. If God can get over it, meaning my sin, then why can't I? God passes the ball, but we refuse to catch it. It happens all the time.

Not to forgive myself does two things to me. First, it is a slap in the face of God and His act of forgiving me. It communicated that God doesn't know what He is doing. Second, to not forgive myself when God has forgiven me is to live a life of defeat. It is to wallow in self-pity and despair. This is far from the life of victory that God wants me to live.

When I was in seminary I had a friend named Mike. Mike was a great guy. A super Christian with a humble spirit. But I always got depressed when Mike prayed. There was a group of us that would meet regularly for prayer and whenever it came Mike's turn to pray, his words would drone on about how filthy and unworthy he was to come before God. He would call himself a worm and proclaim that he was detestable. I have to tell you that it was hard to listen to. I had the sense that Mike really hated himself. I was truly worried about him. I feared that he was living a life of defeat and not victory. There was always dark and never light in his prayers. I think at the core, Mike could not forgive himself even though God could.

Listen friend, this is important. When you ask God to forgive you, He does. End of story. Oh, I'm not talking about some kind of game where you go out on Saturday night and light the town on fire only to show up in church on Sunday to get things "cleaned up." That's just silly and there are a lot of people that play that game. That's what it is, a game. And it's a game that really ticks God off. No, what I am talking about is sincere confession. I'm talking about when you are as disgusted with your sin as God is and you come before Him for forgiveness. When you do that, God forgives. And you should too. *Now get over it…*

Harder to Give than to Receive

I think the biggest struggle that Christians have with forgiveness, though, is the giving of it to others. This is where the Lord's Prayer is more than just a prayer, it is a call to action. Jesus is telling us that we need to be people who forgive.

It is safe to say that most people in the world don't view us Christians as a forgiving bunch. Consider the words of Gary. Gary is just a regular guy who holds a job at a print shop and plays in a band on the weekends. He is married to Erica who has a BA in psychology and works as a counselor. They are in their 30s.[2]

> *"The church is a group of judgmental mudslingers. They seem to really like picking fights with others. Whether it is homosexuals, or other religions, or even with each other. That's the weirdest part. Jesus said to love one another, but you're always hearing how the church fights among themselves and with other denominations. But this isn't anything new. Look at the Crusades. The church has always been an angry bunch."*

There is one more thing you should know about Gary. He grew up in church and now he doesn't go to church anywhere. It's obvious why. You see, when Christians don't forgive, people notice and they leave. Who wants to be around an unforgiving person?

Forgiveness is hard, isn't it? I mean, when someone has done you wrong, hurt you, hurt your family, leveled an insult, stabbed you in the back, it's just hard to turn around and forgive them. Our entire being cries out for revenge. We want to hold a grudge. Friendship is out of the question.

There is something primal within us that wants to hold onto the bitterness. In a sick kind of way, we are comforted by our rage. Go ahead, you can admit it. Unforgiveness feels good. You feel like, in some small fashion, you are balancing the scales. After all, it is up to you to even out all of the world's inequities, right?

If receiving forgiveness is hard, then passing it on to others is ten times harder. It just is. That is why Jesus took time to teach us about forgiveness in something as simple as a prayer. In fact, Jesus is the perfect teacher when it comes to forgiveness. He knows all about being wronged and hurt. He understands what it means to be spat upon and to be betrayed. He knows the pain of having someone talk behind your back. He knows the devastation of people who scheme for your downfall just so they can be lifted up. Jesus understands. He knows forgiveness.

Friendly Fire

Have you ever been wounded by a friend? Have you ever been ambushed by another Christian? Someone within the church? Someone who is supposed to be on your side?

The military reports statistics for causalities in war caused by *friendly fire*. Friendly fire is the result of a phenomenon within the context of battle that is called the "fog of war." When the bullets start flying and soldiers are maneuvering on foot and in machine, things happen fast and it can become very confusing on the battlefield. Unfortunately, the fog of war can lead to friendly fire, where one soldier shoots a comrade thinking he is the enemy, or just purely by accident. Any death in combat is a tragedy, but death by friendly fire has a particularly harsh sting.

Such was the case with Pat Tillman, the famed safety for the Arizona Cardinals drafted by them in 1998. Tillman had been an exceptional scholar athlete. He was named the Pac-

10 Defensive Player of the Year his senior year and he grad-
uated with a GPA of 3.84. Tillman had an instant impact in
the NFL, playing in 10 of 16 games his rookie year. Tillman
was also loyal to his team, at one point turning down a $9
million offer from the St. Louis Rams in order to remain in
Arizona with the team that helped put him on the professional map.

Tillman's loyalty extended far beyond football or his
team. He was also loyal to his country. In the aftermath
of 9/11, Pat Tillman turned down a new contract from the
Cardinals that would have doubled his salary so he could
enlist in the U.S. Army to go and fight for his country.

It's an inspiring story. The kind of stuff movies are
made of. But the story came to a tragic end on April 22,
2004, when while on patrol in Afghanistan, Pat Tillman was
killed by friendly fire. Just like that, it was over. Such talent
and promise. Such heroism and selflessness. All gone in an
instant. He was not killed by the enemy or in some "blaze of
glory" as he took out several members of the opposing force.
No, nothing as Hollywood-esque as that. He was killed by a
fellow soldier. A friend. An accident.

Friendly fire happens all the time in churches. Oh,
nothing as devastating at the story of Pat Tillman, and I in
no way want to equate the pain his family must deal with to
the kind of wounds we inflict on each other within the Body
of Christ.

We Christians have become pretty good at beating up
on each other and, yes, it does hurt. People leave churches,
leave the faith, and sever long-standing relationships, never
to speak to one another again. Even in cases of friendly fire,
we must forgive. I would even say that friendly fire within
the church provides the perfect laboratory to practice the art
of forgiveness, for if you cannot forgive a brother or sister in
Christ, how can you forgive someone who hurts you outside
the church?

A Personal Story

Let me tell you a secret. I've been wounded by people in the church, too. Yes, it's true. Now if you could ever meet me, you'd think that I was such a nice guy, and it would be hard for you to imagine anyone ever wanting to do something to hurt me on purpose! But it's true. I have been the target of intentional friendly fire. When you are being attacked, it's hard to view your attacker as "friendly" even if they are a brother or sister in Christ.

As I mentioned in Act 1 of this book, during my seminary days I pastored a very small, rural church in the extreme northern portion of Texas. We started with about 16 people and grew to about 60 in my 18 months there. Today, Julie and I have the fondest memories of the good people of the Valley View Baptist Church. In so many ways, this city boy was out of place in that country church. But the people were patient with me and they loved me.

There was one lady, in particular, that just didn't like me or my wife. I'll call her Mary although that is not her real name. She lived very close to the church and always knew what time we would show up each weekend and what time we would leave. After a year at the church, I discovered that she was using her influence to spread some pretty ugly rumors and lies about me during the week when I was not there. Word travels quickly in small rural communities, and things got bad fast. What made things so terrible for me personally was that I just could not be there except on the weekends. A rumor started on Monday could fester like a sore by Saturday and Sunday. It could then become infected and pop.

Everything came to a head one particular week when I was attempting to minister to a dear sister in Christ who had just lost her sister to old age. I spent two nights on the phone with this sweet lady praying and consoling her. What

I did not know was that Mary was secretly listening to our conversations on another phone line. She was taking private information from these conversations, twisting what I actually said, then spreading rumors among the people of the church. When I found out what she was doing, I about came unglued. What was the motive? Why would she do this? Why would she add more pain to a situation where death is painful anyway? It made no sense.

I eventually resigned from this church. Partly because of these lies and rumors and partly because it was almost time to graduate and we would be moving on anyway. Needless to say, all the dirty laundry was eventually aired and my reputation was exonerated. I'll never forget our last Sunday at Valley View. After the service was over and we said our tearful goodbyes, a wonderful family took us out for lunch. Over lunch, the husband, Steve, wanted to ask me a question. He asked why I administered the Lord's Supper so often at the church. I thought that was a really unusual question.

Let me give you a little background first. When I first came to Valley View, they observed the Lord's Supper once a quarter like many Baptist churches do. Now, I have a certain affinity for the Lord's Supper. I think it is one of the holiest, most precious moments in the life of a church. Many churches celebrate the Lord's Supper only once a quarter because it can be logistically difficult, especially in larger churches. But Valley View only had 16 people when I arrived. How hard can it be to distribute the elements to 16 people, right? I made the decision to observe the Lord's Supper once a month. My wife even volunteered to wash the little cups and to take care of everything. No one was out anything except the five minutes it took to observe the actual Lord's Supper.

I explained my thinking to Steve and then asked him why it was such a big deal. To my shock, he responded by telling me that for the last year and half, Mary had been telling everyone that the reason I led the church to do the Lord's Supper once a month was because I got extra credit in my seminary classes the more often I did it! Can you believe that? I was floored. It really is amazing what some people *within the church* will do to others. I told Steve that if that was the case, we would have been taking the Lord's Supper every week!

I say all that to say this. I have forgiven Mary. She is my sister in Christ and I love her. I don't understand her, but I love her. I came to the point that I realized that whatever problem she had with me was really more her problem than mine.

I had a friend say to me once something that has forever changed the way I view friendly fire within the church. He said, "Always remember, no human being is really your enemy. For the Christian, our only enemy is Satan." I like that. It helps me to keep things in order. You see, I'll be honest, there are a lot of people I have encountered in church life through the years who bug me, make me mad, and at times, even try to hurt me. As tempting as it is to view them as my enemy, they really aren't. They are my family. Mary really wasn't my enemy. She was my sister. Satan is my enemy, and I suspect that he was roaming around way back then and was the real source of Mary's attacks on me. I don't have it all figured out yet, but I know that one day, Mary and I will sit around together in heaven and talk about all the silly (and at the time hurtful) things we did to each other and just laugh.

The Greatest (and hardest) Commandment

I want to refer back to Gary's quote from just a few pages ago. He is correct when he reminds us that Jesus did say that we should love one another. One day, Jesus was pinned down by a group of men seeking to "trap him in his talk."

They wanted to discredit this new teacher who was growing wildly popular. Jesus was threatening the establishment, so the establishment had to take him down.

The Bible records that after several volleys of conversation, which Jesus won with great ease, a certain scribe came forward to give his best shot. "Jesus," he asked, "what is most the important of all the commandments?" What an interesting question, for the Jews recognized over 600 commandments in the Scriptures. Jesus answered thus,

> *"The most important is, 'Hear, O Israel: The Lord our God, the Lord is one. And you shall love the Lord your God with all your heart and with all your soul and with all your mind and with all your strength.' The second is this: 'You shall love your neighbor as yourself.' There is no other commandment greater than these."*[3]

I love it! I love not only what Jesus said, but the way he said it. Can't you just picture the scene? People pressed in on all sides, watching the match of wits between Israel's finest religious minds and this Jewish carpenter from Nazareth. Nazareth? What good has ever come from Nazareth? The disdain and mockery is thick in the air. And Jesus takes shot after shot and answers without hesitation.

"What's the most important commandant? Love God with all your heart, soul, mind and strength. Oh, and in case you were wondering, the second greatest commandment is to love your neighbor just like you love yourself." Boom! Jesus answers the question and goes one step further. He anticipates the next question and answers it as well. In doing so, Jesus implicates the whole bunch of them who are being neither loving nor very neighborly toward him. The outcome? It says just a few verses later that "after that no one dared ask him any more questions." I love it!

Love, Forgiveness, and Neighbors

Loving and *forgiveness* go hand-in-hand. If you can't love, you can't forgive. And if you can't forgive, you can't love. For God so loved that He gave. Isn't that what John 3:16 says? God was first the great *giver* in order that He could be the great *forgiver*. The whole point of sending His only Son Jesus into the world was so He could have a way to extend forgiveness. He gave and then He forgave.

Love

Let me ask you a question. Do you love people? That is really the beginning point of forgiveness. It is the nature of God to be a lover. He loves you and me with more intensity than we probably will ever understand. There is a reason that the Bible calls the Church the "Bride of Christ." It is the language of a groom madly in love with a woman. She is his bride.

Because it is the nature of God to love people, this love is also in our nature as the restored Image of God. Now I know, people can be hard to love. Trust me, no one knows this better than God. I am ever in awe that God continues to love people in spite of all the ways we reject Him and His love. Which brings up a good point. You can love people and be angry with them at the same time. Just because you love someone does not mean that you won't be disappointed and mad at them. I think about my kids. I love them more than they will probably ever know. But they can sure make me mad. Oh, the stories that I could tell, or any parent can for that matter. The point is that love and anger are not exclusive of each other. You can love people even though you may not like them.

You have to get the loving of people down in your life. If you struggle in this area, ask God to change your heart. Ask Him to beat down the old man in you and to create the new man. But let me warn you, if you pray this way, expect a change. I do not believe that anything is closer to the heart of God than people. That's what it's all about for Him. To be in the image and likeness of God means that people will become close to your heart, too.

Forgiveness

Peter was a hot-head. Peter was stubborn. So stubborn that Jesus nicknamed him "Rocky." Peter was the kind of guy that kept score. If you cut in line, he'd chisel it into the record book of his stony mind. Peter was also one to settle a score. He could only take so much. If you cut him off with your chariot on the highway, he'd probably respond with road rage and shoot an arrow at you. Remember, this is the guy who cut people's ears off. A regular Mike Tyson. Rocky.

One day, Peter just had to know. "Lord, how often will my brother sin against me, and I forgive him? Seven times?" Can't you just see Peter? I mean, he's really bent out of shape on this one. This question didn't just come out of a vacuum. Something had happened. Peter was ticked. He'd been following Jesus around, listening to his teaching, learning all about love and forgiveness. But come on, there has to be a limit, right? I mean, we aren't expected to just *take it,* are we?

If I were guessing, I'd say that Peter and another one of the disciples had been mixing it up. After all, he called him *brother.* Let's face it, if you travel with, eat with, camp out with a group of guys long enough, somebody is going to eventually get on your nerves. Words will be exchanged and blows will be traded. This happens in the church all the time. This is what Gary was talking about a few pages back: church people always fighting with one another. It happens every week in churches all across the country. Peter wants to know how much is enough. He takes his question all the way to the top.

Here is the question that Peter was really asking and that you and I ask all the time: *Is there a limit to forgiveness?*

It's a good question if you think about it. In a world where so much wrong is done by one person or group of people toward each other, it's a good question. Can we really forgive a guy like Jeffrey Dahmer who kidnapped, raped, murdered and cannibalized 17 men and boys? Or what about those Islamic extremists who hijacked American planes and flew them into buildings on 9/11, killing 3,000 people? This is where forgiveness becomes a hard pass to throw. These kinds of things happen all the time in our world. They always have and they always will. Do I really have to forgive, and do they even deserve it? *Is there a limit to forgiveness?*

How did Jesus respond? He told Peter a story, a parable. The story goes like this.[4] There once was a king who decided to settle his accounts with his servants. One particular servant owed the king a lot of money, ten thousand talents to be exact. The king knew the servant could not repay him so he ordered that the servant, along with his wife and kids, be sold as slaves in order to settle the account. Upon hearing this, the servant fell on his knees and begged for mercy. The king was a very good king and was moved by this display of humility. He forgave the servant his debt and sent him on his way.

That's part one of the story. Part two is where it gets interesting. The servant left the presence of the king and immediately went to one of his friends, a fellow servant, who owed him money. Three hundred denarri was the debt. The servant who had just had his own debt forgiven demanded immediate payment from his friend. When his friend could not pay, he grabbed him and began choking him. The man begged for mercy but got none. Instead, he was ordered thrown into prison until he could scrape together the funds. Interesting, huh? Now for the finale.

There were witnesses to parts one and two of our story. You see, there are always witnesses. We may think that our actions are unseen, but they aren't. People always know. Who you really are will always be found out. Well, these witnesses were obviously disturbed by the events that had unfolded, so they went to the king to tell him what had transpired. The king was furious. He called the servant he had forgiven back into his chamber and let him have it. "I can't believe I forgave you, but you could not forgive someone else!" He ordered the servant thrown into his own jail cell until he could raise the money to pay his debt.

Jesus then closed this story by looking at Peter, and probably the rest of the disciples, and said, "So also my heavenly Father will do to every one of you, if you do not forgive your brother from your heart."

Good story. But let's dig just a little deeper. To fully understand the implications of this parable, you need to understand the size of the debt that was owed by each servant. Remember, the real question that Peter was asking was whether or not there is a limit to forgiveness. In other words, can a debt ever be so high that it should be repaid rather than forgiven?

Remember that the first servant owed the king ten thousand talents. It's hard to know how much money that is because we don't use talents and denarii in our currency system today. We need to do a little converting to dollars to make sense of this.

A denarious was one of the lowest sums of money in the Roman currency system. One denarious was considered one day's worth of wages for a blue collar worker. How much is that? Well, the minimum wage is currently $6.55 per hour. If the average employee works eight hours a day, then one denarious would be around $52. A talent was a much larger sum of money. So large that it took 6,000 denarii to equal just one talent. That means that one talent would be around $312,000. Now that's big money. If you owed someone $312,000 it would take you quite a while to pay that back. If that is what you paid for a home, you'd be looking at a 30-year mortgage.

Remember that the first servant owed his king ten thousand talents. You're starting to understand, aren't you? Go ahead and do the math. Ten thousand talents would be $3,120,000,000. That's more than three billion dollars! That's absurd, isn't it? That's an impossible amount to pay back. *That* is Jesus' point. It's *supposed* to be an impossible amount. You can just hear the disciples laughing as Jesus tells the story. Everyone knows that he is using a crazy amount of money to prove a very serious point. For one, a servant would never be able to borrow that kind of money from a king, much less pay it back. Also notice that Jesus makes the point of telling us that it was a king that the money was borrowed from, not just your average employer. You see, only a king could forgive such an outrageous debt.

Now contrast the one servant who was just forgiven a debt of over three billion dollars, who in turn had a debt of 300 denarii owed to him. That's just over $15,000 in today's dollars. A lot of money for sure, but certainly not an impossible amount. This man cannot forgive $15,000 when he was just forgiven three billion. Amazing, isn't it?

Jesus' final point was dead-pan serious. "Peter," he said, "there is no limit to forgiveness. Further, the man who refuses to forgive will find himself in a prison of his own making."

Don't miss that last point. Forgiveness is tough, but lack of forgiveness is slavery. Slavery to your own bitterness, anger, and pride. It is a prison cell of which you will never be able to escape. For if you can't forgive others, then you don't deserve forgiveness yourself. You have to repay your own debts back to the King. Debts that are far beyond any sum owed to you. Debts that exceed far beyond your ability to repay. Outrageous debts that only a King can forgive.

Neighbors

There is no limit to forgiveness. As Christians we must be a forgiving people. Of *all* offenses for which forgiveness is sought. Perhaps even grant forgiveness, in some cases, where forgiveness is *not* sought. You see, forgiveness is really as much, if not more, about our own spiritual, emotional, and psychological well-being as it is the offender's.

The next question that flows from this whole discussion on forgiveness is this: *Who exactly is my neighbor?*

There is a wonderful passage of Scripture in the book of Luke where this very question is put to Jesus.[5] We are told that one day a lawyer approached Jesus. Okay, not to make fun, but this *is* funny. It's just like a lawyer to be looking for a loophole, isn't it? The story begins in such a way that it sounds like the start of a bad joke. But it's no joke. A lawyer really did approach Jesus and he wanted to know how to receive eternal life. By all accounts this man was sincere. Not like the scribe we saw earlier who was trying "catch" Jesus in some guffaw. This man really wanted to know how to get to heaven. Jesus responded by saying that you must obey God's Law, and then he asked the lawyer what his interpretation of the Law was. Once again Jesus was speaking the language of the audience. A *lawyer* had a question so Jesus talked about the *Law*.

It is obvious that this man had been following Jesus for some time and listening to him teach, because his answer was a quote from Jesus himself. "You shall love the Lord your God with all your heart and with all your soul and with all your strength and with all your mind, and your neighbor as yourself," said the attorney.

Jesus was pleased. He liked the answer. It was his answer after all. He encouraged the lawyer to go his way and practice this interpretation of the Law. But the lawyer was not done. He was a lawyer, remember? "Uh, one more question, Jesus. Who exactly is my neighbor?" Don't you love it? You see, forgiveness is hard. We just don't want to do it. We'd rather hold on and become a slave to our rage. If I only have to love and forgive my neighbor, then doesn't that mean that I don't have to love and forgive my non-neighbor?

What did Jesus do? What did Jesus always do? He told another story. This time it was a story about a man who was robbed while traveling on a treacherous stretch of highway. The man was not only robbed, but stripped, beaten and left to die. The man was a Jew. That's important. The text says he was traveling from Jerusalem to Jericho, two Jewish cities.

As the story continues, two very religious men came by at different times. A priest first, and later a Levite. Both of these men would have recognized the injured man as a Jew because of his circumcision (remember, he was naked). If ever there was a neighbor, it would be one Jew to another. But both of these religious Jews continued on without helping the man, each for his own reasons.

And then a Samaritan happened by. Here's what you need to know, Samaritans and Jews hated each other. I mean they really hated each other. Samaritans were considered half-breeds by the Jews. Half Jewish blood and half foreign blood. The Jews would go out of their way to abuse and make life miserable for the Samaritans. As a result, the Samaritans despised the Jews. It would not be so unlike a Palestinian running upon a car wreck in Israel today where the driver was a Jew found bleeding to death.

Did the Samaritan abandon the Jew? He had every reason to. He *was* a Jew, for one. No one would blame him. They certainly weren't neighbors! Further, it would have been very risky for the Samaritan to stop and take care of a Jew.

What if he died while the Samaritan was trying to help? He would easily be seen as causing his death and thus his own life would be on the line. This was Jewish country after all. But the Samaritan did stop. And he did help. He went above and beyond mere first-aid. He carried the man to the nearest town, left the inn keeper $100, and left instructions to put any additional charges on his personal account.

Jesus then looked the lawyer square in the eye and asked him a question. "You tell me, Mr. Attorney. Who do you think was the neighbor of the man who was robbed and left for dead?" The answer is obvious, isn't it? It was obvious to the attorney.

You see, even your enemy is your neighbor.

Miracle on the River Kwai

Several years ago I was exposed to the story of Ernest Gordon. Gordon's story has had a profound and lasting impact on my life in ways that few stories have ever touched me. I had heard that a movie by Christian director David Cunningham was being released. The movie was to be an adaptation of Ernest Gordon's account of life as a POW in a Japanese prison camp during World War II. I love war movies and so I was intrigued. When I heard that Gordon had written a book that was the basis of the screenplay, I ordered a copy. The title of the book was the same as the title of the movie, *To End All Wars*. What I read was powerful and moving. When I eventually saw the movie, I was equally as moved.[6]

Ernest Gordon was a Scottish soldier of the Argyll and Southerland Highlanders. Captured at sea, Gordon was ferried off to Thailand where he eventually was made part of the forced labor crew that built what would come to be known as the Railroad of Death. This 415 kilometer route was constructed for the purpose of transporting Japanese military supplies between Thailand and Burma. The railroad crossed the Kwai Yai River. This became the inspiration for the famous 1957 film *The Bridge on the River Kwai*, directed by David Lean and starring Alec Guiness and William Holden. This movie was a highly romanticized version of the true story. Gordon wanted it made known that while it may be a good movie, the story it tells is nowhere near the reality of life and death that he experienced as a Japanese prisoner.

The Railroad of Death was such named because of the human toll it exacted on the slave work force "commissioned" by the Japanese. Sixty-thousand Allied soldiers were forced into labor along with 270,000 Asian workers, a clear violation of the Geneva Convention. They were required to work tirelessly with little to no food and water. They were given no clothing other than what they brought into captivity. As those clothes rotted on their bodies, they just had to make do.

The Japanese were known for being harsh and cruel. They viewed their prisoners as less valuable than animals and treated them as such. The workforce suffered inhuman cruelties as they hacked their way through malarial swamps, over mountains and across rivers, laying mile after mile of railroad track. As a result, over 80,000 men died to lay this Railroad of Death. That's approximately 393 lives per mile of track. Unbelievable.

Ernest Gordon's personal story is one that took him to the brink of death himself. Severely malnourished, Gordon developed Beri Beri. Additionally, he contracted malaria and a jungle ulcer. In one horrific episode, he underwent surgery to remove a bad kidney without anesthesia or pain medication. Gordon became so sick that he was consigned to the Death House, a larger hut where the dead and soon-to-die were placed. This was Gordon's lowest point.

In the midst of this inhumanity, two men befriended this poor Scot and humanely began to nurse him back to care. These two friends were Dusty Miller and "Dinty" Moore. Dusty was a Methodist and Dinty a Roman Catholic. Both men sacrificed their own rations to provide extra food for Ernest. They would boil rags and change the dressings on his wounds daily. Ernest had become paralyzed in his legs and could not even walk for an extended period. But over time, his health improved and so did his spirits.

Ernest Gordon went into captivity an agnostic, not sure what he believed when it came to God. But what he saw in these two men, the love of Christ expressed verbally and with actions, changed him. He gave his life to Christ.

As the three-and-a-half years of imprisonment took their toll, some men became barbarians, stealing and turning on their fellow man out of sheer self-preservation. Yet, others refused to lose their sense of humanity. They held on to their dignity as the Image of God.

A "college" of sorts was formed where trained prisoners would teach the untrained. Gordon tells of the "church without walls" that was formed in the jungle. There was no need of a fence to contain the prisoners, for escape would mean certain death in the jungle. The men would secretly meet and worship and read portions of the Bible if they had them. In one moving scene in the movie, the prisoners formed a type of orchestra with homemade instruments of bamboo and string. They even held a performance for their Japanese captors.

The cruelty of the Japanese military was relentless. Gordon recalls an occasion when four men tried to escape. They were caught, beaten and shot in the head in front of the rest of the camp during role call. This was to send a message of what would happen to those who disobeyed the will of the Emperor of Japan. In another appalling story, a shovel turned up missing in the daily tool count. A man stepped forward to take responsibility and was beaten to the point of being paralyzed from the waste down – only to later discover that there had been a miscount. The shovel was never missing.

But most devastating to Gordon was the execution of his Christian brother, Dusty Miller. Dusty's faith incited the ire of a Japanese guard who simply could not tolerate his sense of calm in the midst of such hardship. Just two weeks prior to the end of the war, the soldier hauled Dusty outside the camp and crucified him on a tree. Additionally, Gordon would discover that Dinty Moore had also died in captivity. Yet, somehow, against all odds, Ernest Gordon had survived.

After the war, Ernest Gordon moved to the United States and went on to become the Dean of the Chapel at Princeton University where he served for 26 years. He died on January 16, 2002, just two years after his story was told as a major motion picture. As part of the filming of *To End All Wars*, the producers had arranged a ceremony of reconciliation. Ernest, along with his son, Alastair, were flown from New York to Thailand, and later driven to the Kanchanaburi War Cemetery. The cemetery is the resting place of 6,982 Allied soldiers who died on the Railroad of Death.

Arrangements had been made for Ernest Gordon to be "reunited" with Nagase Takashi, a former Japanese officer who had served as an interpreter on the Burma-Thailand Railroad. It would be the first time these two men had come face-to-face since the war. The film crew caught the whole reunion on camera, allowing us to witness the event as it unfolded.

Although it is February, it is obvious on film that it is a hot and humid day. As Gordon and Takashi meet at the marble arch of the cemetery's entry gate, Takashi takes Gordon's hand and shakes it. The former Japanese captor apologizes to Gordon for the atrocities committed by his fellow Japanese. And what does Ernest Gordon do?

He forgives him.

The two men walk together through the rows of headstones, talking and commenting on the names. At the far end of the cemetery, they lay a wreath of flowers. In a small but moving gesture, Takashi, who is holding an umbrella, is careful to place it over Gordon as well, to provide relief from the sun's rays. You can view the whole scene on the DVD just before the credit role. But I warn you, it will make you cry.

Is there a limit to forgiveness?

No.

Who is my neighbor?

Even my enemy is my neighbor.

Chapter 9 – Body

The Church gets a bad rap today. It is the target of those on the outside and those on the inside. It is easy to find people who are down on Church. You don't have to travel very far to find someone who is put out with Church, or someone who used to go to a church and doesn't anymore and has some horror story to tell about why they left.

I'll be the first to admit that the Church is not perfect. I know this to be true primarily because I am a member of the Church. I know all too well my own imperfections. I once heard it said that if I ever found the perfect church, I shouldn't join it because as soon as I did, it would cease to be that way. Oh, how true. I think we would all do well to keep those words of advice in mind.

I hear people all the time say that they don't want to be a part of any church because churches are full of hypocrites. I'll bet you've heard that one, too. My response to that particular charge is, "Yeh, so what?" Tell me something I don't know. All people are sinners. We established that in chapter one. That means all people. Yes, there are hypocrites in churches along with liars, thieves, porn addicts, gamblers, men who hit their kids, and probably every other kind of sin, most of which we don't want to know about.

Incidentally, there are hypocrites, liars, thieves, porn addicts, gamblers, abusive men, etc. that live in your neighborhood, too. So what are you going to do? Move out? Move to another neighborhood where you won't be around those kinds of people? Good luck. You see, churches are full of the same kinds of people that are in the world. I don't know of any church that claims to be perfect (although I have met a few Christians that act like they are!). The *reason* a group of sinners, that contain hypocrites and liars and all the rest, come together in the form of a church, is significant. It is essential to realizing the restored Image of God.

We have much to talk about, don't we? One thing for sure is that everyone, those in churches and those outside churches, have definite and strong opinions about what the Church is and what it isn't and what it should be. Let's begin by defining what exactly a church is.

Church 101

Very simply, the Church is people. More specifically, the Church is people who are Christians. I hate to break the news to some of you, but if you have surrendered your life to Christ and become one of His followers, you are a member of His Church. I use a capital letter "C" here because in one sense, the Church is universal. It is made up of all followers of Jesus who live all around the world: past, present, and future. Paul speaks in Hebrews of being surrounded by a "great cloud of witnesses." It's a description of those followers of God who have gone before, and who are cheering for us today as we run the race.[1] This is the Church. If you're saved, you're in. Congratulations and welcome!

The Church is broken into smaller groups that meet together. These are the local churches listed in your phonebook. I use the small letter "c" when I talk about these churches. Once again, the church, just like the Church, is people. While all Christians are members of *the* Church, not all Christians are members of *a* church. This is true for all kinds of reasons, some of which I have already touched on.

The People Factor

I really cannot stress enough the importance of coming to terms with the truth that the Church and the church are all about people. I say that because in America, we tend to think of a church as a building. What's ironic is that church people are the worst about this. The unchurched seem to understand this concept better than those who attend church. As I said, the reason many people don't go to church is because of the people in the church, not the building. The criticisms that the unchurched level at the church are most always about the people, not the facilities. In fact, I have never met anyone who gave up on church because the building just didn't meet their needs. It always comes back to the people.

We church people love our buildings. We take great pride in them. A group of people get together to form a church, and the first item on the agenda is to find property and start a building campaign. Oh sure, if you ask them what a church is they'll say it's people, but their actions indicate something else. There are more church fights over buildings than probably any other topic. "Do we build or not build?" "How big or how small should we build?" "Should we go into debt or not to go into debt?" "How much debt should we incur?" I won't even go into the litany of items related to the building that people will argue and fight about. Once the building is built, it becomes sacred. God forbid we should tear down a wall, or even the whole building. And please, no, don't bring up the R-word – *relocate*. "That building was built by my grandfather." "My dad was one of the actual framers of the education building." You get the idea, don't you?

Too many churches define themselves by facilities and not people. This is simply not God's way. Here's something to think about. If your church was to burn down tonight, and your pastor called and said that everyone was meeting at the Holiday Inn on Friday night for worship because that's the only night the hotel was available, how many people do you think would show up? The ones who would are the ones who get it. It's all about people.

Our churches today could use a good dose of doctrine on what the church is and what it isn't. I think we know it in our heads, but we get hung up in practice. Remember the church without walls from the last chapter? Last year I showed my church a picture of a tree in Africa and asked them if they knew what it was. They said, "Sure, it's a tree." I said, "No, it's a church." That particular tree was where a church of people met. I asked them what would happen to the church if the tree were struck by lightening and burned down. Without hesitation, they said the people would just move to another tree. Why is this so easy to grasp when it is some other group in some other country, but hard to grasp when it is *my* church in *my* country?

I was greatly impressed when I read that Rick Warren's church met for over ten years before they ever built their first building. Today, Saddleback Community Church is the largest local church in the United States. That church gets it. It's all about people.

I think if I were going to start a church from scratch today, I would delay building anything as long as possible. In fact, more and more churches are doing this today than ever before. Intentionally not constructing a building. Meeting in schools and theatres and hotels. Does that bother you? Why? "For where two or three are gathered in my name, there I am among them."[2] It was Jesus who said that, by the way. Do we believe it or not?

Dependence Day

The Fourth of July is Independence Day in the United States. Each year we gather in groups to eat burgers and hot dogs, to blow things up, and to celebrate our break away from the King of England. The independence of our nation is something that we as Americans hold very dear. The pioneer mindset runs deep in the blood of who we are. We love to celebrate the individual.

This independent spirit runs contrary to who we are as believers in Jesus Christ. In fact, you must surrender your independence to even become a Christian. For Christ to be the King and Ruler of your life, you must let go of self. The day that you become a Christian is your Dependence Day. You are saying that from this day forward, you need Jesus. You can't do it by yourself.

Jesus has put in place a support system to sustain and grow you, to help restore you to the Image of God. That support system involves two important elements. First, there is the Holy Spirit. After his resurrection, Jesus promised his followers that even though he was going away, he would send them a Helper. On the day of Pentecost the Holy Spirit descended to indwell believers and to empower them. The Holy Spirit works on you as an individual because there is most definitely an individual aspect to faith in Christ. It is the Holy Spirit that gives every believer at least one spiritual gift. It is the Holy Spirit that leads the believer to understand and interpret the words of the Bible. And it is the Holy Spirit that guides and bends the heart and mind of the believer so that they may know the will of God.

There is a second element to this support system that Jesus put into place for us. That second element is the church. Now, as I stated, once you become a believer, you are already a part of the Church universal, but it is absolutely critical that you find and become an active member of a local church.

Very frequently I hear people say that their Christianity is private. "I worship God in my home." Or, "I don't need a church to be close to God or to pray to Jesus." This kind of attitude is the hottest thing going right now. As I said I hear it *all* the time. You've probably heard it too. My response is very simple. YES, you should worship God in your home and YES, there is definitely a private aspect to your faith that you should practice. But NO, your Christianity is not altogether private. Christ demands that your faith be *public* and shared *corporately*.

Jesus never intended for you to keep your faith to yourself. He was very clear in the gospel of Matthew that your faith should be publicly declared. In fact, Jesus went as far as to say that if you are unwilling to declare your faith publicly, then you really aren't a Christian at all.[3]

The Bible is clear that the individual believer was meant to come together with other believers in corporate worship. This is the part that so many people get hung up on today. I want you to listen very carefully to me on this point, *the Christian life was never meant to be walked alone.* I would even go as far as to say that the Christian life walked alone is not the Christian life at all. The Christian life is not one of independence, but of dependence. I think that is especially hard for those of us who are Americans, because the independent mindset is so deeply ingrained into the fabric of our nation and our culture. As Christians, we must come to understand that we are citizens of the heavenly Kingdom first, and citizens of an earthly kingdom second.

A Theology of Community

Think about this. Even within the God-head, there is dependence. God is One, but that One is expressed in the

Holy Trinity. Father, Son, and Holy Spirit. God is One and Three. He is independent and dependent. Doesn't it make sense that the Image of God would function the same way?

God created us for community. The Image of God is a collective. That is what I mean when I say that you cannot fully function as the restored Image of God unless you are part of a church. That's the way God set it up. To reject the church is to reject the Image of God. It is, in reality, a slam on God Himself. Many people never understand this.

For better or for worse, you need to be a part of a church. I don't care if there are hypocrites there or not. Those people are the Image of God as well. Before you get too critical, go check yourself in a mirror first. Don't worry about the speck in someone else's eye when you've got a 2x4 in your own.

God never intended for us to walk through life alone. He always intended for us to live in community.

I love theology. I have many books on the subject. One of my favorite books is by Stanley Grenz. I love the title of his systematic theology text, *Theology for the Community of God*. That's what I'm talking about. The word *theology* means the study of God. There is something profoundly godly about living the Christian life in community with other believers. Look at what the writer of Hebrews charged the believers of his day with,

> *And let us consider how to stir up one another to love and good works, not neglecting to meet together, as is the habit of some, but encouraging one another, and all the more as you see the Day drawing near.*[4]

This passage makes it very clear. We are told to not neglect meeting together. It points out that this had become a habit for some believers in the first century just as it has for people in our day.

I'm certainly not saying the church gets it right all the time. There are certain things we ought to be doing when we come together. The passage above mentions a couple of reasons we need each other. We need to "stir" each other up to love and good works. I like the way that is phrased. I know, and have been a part of, churches that stir things up but not the kind of things the writer of Hebrews is talking about.

We should also encourage each other. Nobody likes to be beat up. Too many times, people show up at church and walk away feeling like a pin-cushion; like people have been poking holes in them all morning long. Yes, I know it happens and it is wrong. That kind of junk needs to be done away with. But even if the church you are a part of stirs up trouble and hurts people, that is no reason to run away.

I had a church member come to me recently and tell me that she just loves our church and all the things going on in it. She has a few friends that are always critical of the church and complaining about it. She asked me what she should say to them. I told her to tell them what she just told me! Tell them you love your church and have no clue what they're talking about. Nothing will squash negativity quicker than someone who is positive. If nothing else, that person won't come to you with their gripes anymore. Too many times, the people who love their church (which in my experience is the majority) are silenced by the few negative people that are in all churches. So don't be silent. Stand up for your church and be heard. Stand up for the community of God.

For the Love of Christ

There is something just profoundly wrong-headed and nonsensical about the person who claims to be a Christian and to love Jesus, but then turns around and rejects the church outright. If you love someone, and I mean truly love them, you are also going to love what they love.

I love my wife. I mean, I *really* love my wife. My love for Julie has changed my loves and desires. Because of her, I will watch a chick-flick; and shhh, don't tell anyone, but I will actually kind of like it. I wouldn't want to watch a chick-flick with anyone else, though. Left to myself I'd rather watch a war movie or a good Western.

Before I met Julie I hated vegetables. My wife loves vegetables and she loves to cook and she's a very good cook. So guess what, I have come to love vegetables. Maybe not as much as her, but I eat them and actually sort of like them now...even broccoli.

If you say you love Jesus and you really mean it, then you are going to love what he loves. And what does Jesus love?

His Bride.

That's right. Just like I love my bride, and if you're a guy the way that you love your bride, Jesus loves *his* Bride. The Bible calls the Church the Bride of Christ. The Bible does this on purpose because this is love language!

My parents love me and so they love Julie, my wife. Julie's parents love her and so they love me now, too. True love can cause you to look past a lot of blemishes for the sake of love.

Listen, Jesus loves the Church, his Bride. I want to show you something. The book of Revelation is one of the most beautiful books in all of the Bible. I recently took more than half a year and preached through the whole book. It had a profound impact on my life. The book of Revelation is really most accurately titled *The Revelation of Jesus Christ*. In fact, those are the first five words of the book. This book is a vision of Jesus, a revealing of him, to the disciple John. John was told to write it all down and to send it to the seven major churches of his day. Those seven churches served as a distribution network to spread this revelation to all churches and eventually to us today.

When you read the book of Revelation, you see Jesus in his full glory. It is an amazing thing to see. In the first chapter we see Jesus in a way we never saw him in the gospel accounts. Read this for yourself and be amazed,

> *Then I turned to see the voice that was speaking to me, and on turning I saw seven golden lampstands, and in the midst of the lampstands one like a son of man, clothed with a long robe and with a golden sash around his chest. The hairs of his head were white like wool, as white as snow. His eyes were like a flame of fire, his feet were like burnished bronze, refined in a furnace, and his voice was like the roar of many waters. In his right hand he held seven stars, from his mouth came a sharp two-edged sword, and his face was like the sun shining in full strength.*[5]

Impressive, isn't it?! As you read these words, you realize that you are witnessing Royalty. The Son of God revealed in all his glory. The Lion of Judah. The King of Kings. It will give you goose bumps. Notice what surrounds Jesus. Seven golden lampstands. Jesus will declare just a few verses later that these lampstands are the seven churches to which this vision will be sent. Isn't it interesting and telling that Jesus surrounds himself with his churches? You see, Jesus *loves* the Church, his Church, his churches.

If you read on, you'll see that these were not perfect churches. Far from it, they had some real problems and Jesus calls them on the carpet. He says it like it is. I'd even go as far as to say that these churches had hypocrites in them. None of this, not the problems or the hypocrites, ever affected Jesus' love for his Bride.

That is why I say that you can't claim to love Jesus and then say you don't want anything to do with his Church. For the love of Christ you must love the Church.

Body Language

The Bible also refers to the Church as the Body of Christ. That is interesting language, but it is also a powerful and intentional metaphor given to us by Scripture. I have included here a passage from 1 Corinthians 12:12-26. It is long but I want you to read the whole thing because it says so plainly what I am going to elaborate on in the next few paragraphs.

For just as the body is one and has many members, and all the members of the body, though many, are one body, so it is with Christ. For in one Spirit we were all baptized into one body— Jews or Greeks, slaves or free—and all were made to drink of one Spirit. For the body does not consist of one member but of many. If the foot should say, "Because I am not a hand, I do not belong to the body," that would not make it any less a part of the body. And if the ear should say, "Because I am not an eye, I do not belong to the body," that would not make it any less a part of the body. If the whole body were an eye, where would be the sense of hearing? If the whole body were an ear, where would be the sense of smell? But as it is, God arranged the members in the body, each one of them, as he chose. If all were a single member, where would the body be? As it is, there are many parts, yet one body. The eye cannot say to the hand, "I have no need of you," nor again the head to the feet, "I have no need of you." On the contrary, the parts of the body that seem to be weaker are indispensable, and on those parts of the body that we think less honorable we bestow the greater honor, and our unpresentable parts are treated with greater modesty, which our more presentable parts do not require. But God has so composed the body, giving greater honor to the part that lacked it, that there may be no division in the body, but that the members may have the same care for one another. If one member suffers, all suffer together; if one member is honored, all rejoice together.

You are a part of the Body. This language of Body emphasizes the idea of community. The Body functions and works together. When any portion of the Body is amputated, that is never good. The picture of a missing foot or hand is tragic. Can you see how silly it is now to say that you can live out your faith as a Christian without the church? What good is a foot unless it is attached to the body? Yet, people are convinced that they can actually function and be what God wants them to be even though they are severed from the Body. It just makes no sense.

Notice also that this Body language also emphasizes the importance of all parts of the Body. I have a problem with warts on my left knee. That's probably way more than you wanted to know about me, but I do have a point so please keep reading.

This morning I opened one of those "at-home" kits for freezing warts. I've done this before so I knew what to expect. I froze this little Q-tip type device that came in the kit and then touched it to four places on my knee where I have small warts. Sitting here writing this chapter about four hours later, my knee feels like it is on fire. These are just tiny spots, but they are making my whole knee and mid-leg ache. In fact, my whole body is affected. It's hard not to walk funny because my pants rub against the spots and walking really intensifies the pain. Isn't it funny how that works? Something as ordinary as walking across the room becomes extra-ordinary because a small insignificant spot on my body is in pain.

I'm sure you've had the same experience. Maybe it was a hang nail, or a crick in your neck, or wound on your arm. All of a sudden the simple becomes difficult and your whole body reacts. You see, there are no insignificant parts to your body. If I held you down and ripped your pinky toenail out, all of a sudden a part of your body that you rarely think about becomes the focus of your attention. And the whole body suffers.

This is why Body language is so powerful when it comes to talking about the church. There are no insignificant people in the church. Everybody counts. If anyone suffers, we all suffer. If anyone rejoices, we all rejoice. That's the way it works. If you have ever thought you were small and insignificant in your church, then stop thinking that way.

No Unimportant Parts

We work very hard at the church I pastor to instill significance into every role our people fill. For instance, we have a parking lot ministry. Doesn't sound too glamorous, does it? Our parking lot team is a part of our overall First Impressions Ministry. We believe that first impressions count for a lot.

If you go to a restaurant for the first time and have a bad experience, not only will you never go back, but you are sure to tell everyone. My wife and I went to *Bennigan's* years ago for dinner with some friends. When our food was being delivered, the waiter spilled an entire glass of tea on my friend Danny. He was drenched. They brought towels to clean up everything, but they still made him pay for his dinner. We couldn't believe they didn't offer to comp his meal, which is standard practice in many restaurants.

At the same meal, my wife ordered chicken that called for melted cheese on top. When her food arrived, the chicken was not cooked all the way through. Rather than cooking her a new chicken breast, they put that same one, cheese and all, back on the grill to finish cooking it. When it came back, the cheese was burned and the chicken was overcooked. The whole thing was a bad experience. A very bad first impression. This all happened years ago and I still remember the details. Over the years we have told many people about our experience. Sure, I know that overall *Bennigan's* is probably a fine restaurant. Maybe just the one we went to had a bad spell with management or help or whatever, but my point is that first impressions matter.

From our church's perspective, we have put great value on our parking lot team. They are the first people with which a guest will have contact. That contact begins before words are spoken as people unfamiliar with our campus are trying to find a place to park. The contact continues with a warm smile and easy-to-understand information on where to drop off kids or find a Bible study class. If it's raining, an umbrella offered doesn't hurt either. We have placed this kind of value on all our people no matter what they do: opening doors, changing diapers, handing out bulletins, escorting guests, etc.

Dear reader, you are important. You are part of the Body. If you are playing Lone Ranger with your Christian walk, that means some church in your town is being robbed and deprived of what you can add to them. They are suffering without you. They need you. There are no insignificant parts to the Body.

Occasionally, people leave my church. I hate it. I hate to lose people. People leave for all kinds of reasons, but mostly because they just don't like the way things are going. Whenever I talk to them I encourage them to be sure to find another church where they do agree with the way things are going. And then dive into that church. Make a contribution. They have so much to offer the Body. If not here, then down the road at another church. After all, it really is one Body and one Church.

I Wanna Do Church Like They Did It in the New Testament

This is a sentiment that is growing today. With the advent of the emerging church movement, the spotlight has been cast on the discontent that many people have in the "institution" of the church. By "institution" I mean what most people think of when they think of church: a group of people who meet regularly in a building, who have a pastor or pastors, and who have an ad in the phone book.

The institution of the church has come under some serious fire lately by those who claim that virtually everything the church does is unbiblical. These people then call for a return to doing church the way they did it in the New Testament.

One of the chief proponents of this mindset is Frank Viola who has recently been joined by George Barna in a collaborative book called *Pagan Christianity?* Viola is a major player in the house church movement and appears to be the primary voice behind much of what is said in the book. Barna is the founder and director of The Barna Group, which is a Christian research and resource firm. This book caught my attention because I have historically loved Barna's work. He has contributed greatly to describing where the Church and Christians are in terms of the culture and attitudes about the faith from both those inside and outside. But by coupling with Viola, Barna has crossed over from being *descriptive* to being *prescriptive* in his work. Because of his level of influence, I am concerned.

I don't mean to be attacking of Viola or Barna. I have never met either one of them but from what I know of them through their writings, they both seem to be very sincere and godly men. They are my brothers in Christ. But I don't agree with their *prescriptive* diagnosis of institutional churches. They are both a good example of, as I said, the growing sentiment that the institution of the church has got it all wrong and that we need a return, or a reformation, back to the way church was intended to be as described in the New Testament. They see virtually every facet of the institution of the church as unbiblical, and in the words of Viola and Barna, rooted in paganism. This includes the existence of the pastor as most people think of him, the existence of a worship minister, the use of buildings and property owned by a church, tithing, the sermon, paid clergy, and it goes on and on. The claim that is made is that all of it is unbiblical.[6]

The New Testament Church

When someone says to me that they think we need to get back to doing church the way they did it in the New Testament, my response is, "Which New Testament church?" My question is usually met with a funny stare. They then ask me a question, "What do you mean?"

For some reason, people tend to think that there was just one New Testament church. Nothing could be further from the truth. The first church was in Jerusalem and you can read about it in the book of Acts. You can also read about the missionary journeys of Paul and Barnabas whereby they traveled around Asia Minor planting churches everywhere they went.

I don't know about you, but even in my own town today, there are no two churches that are the same. I pastor a Southern Baptist Church and have been a member of the Southern Baptist denomination my whole life. I can assure you that no two Southern Baptist churches are the same. Oh, sure there are similarities, but there are also great differences.

In the church I currently pastor, we have a Board of Overseers that holds me accountable, but we are essentially a pastor-led church. I know other Southern Baptist churches that are led by a deacon body. That's a big difference. In the church I pastor, we hardly ever use an organ on Sunday mornings anymore, but in another Southern Baptist church just down the road, they use an organ every Sunday. Trust me, there is a big difference in our worship styles because of this.

In addition, the changing of the times changes the way churches do church. A couple of generations ago, a church's only access to a pastor might be a circuit preacher who would travel to two or more churches in the course of a month, preaching and ministering to the congregations on different Sundays. This was not completely unlike Paul's pastoring of the churches he planted through return trips and the letters of the New Testament. Today, most churches have their own pastors. It is a choice they make individually based on desire and ability. But change continues. Whereas we had circuit preachers in the past, today we are seeing the advent of closed-circuit preachers: pastors who preach live in one location, and also preach via simulcast video to multiple other churches at the same time.

Now, you would never be able to say that video preaching is "biblical" because they never even had that technology in the New Testament. Neither does that mean that video preaching is "unbiblical." I guess if you want, you could say that video preaching has pagan origins since a "pagan" invented video broadcasting. Does that mean the church can't or shouldn't utilize that technology to spread the gospel?

This is where I think we have to be very careful about claiming the biblical high ground in terms of what the Bible says about how a church should be conducted and operated and structured. What we see in the Bible is a *description* of what the church looked like at its beginnings. Not a *prescription* of what it should be for all times.

I mentioned the first church in Acts located in the city of Jerusalem. This church is *described* as meeting daily and selling all their possessions and putting everything in a community pot. I have heard people say that is what we should to do today in order to be like the New Testament church. But there is no indication that this kind of behavior lasted very long. In fact, I think you can make a strong argument that when we see this same church in Jerusalem many years later in the book of Acts, they have ceased this practice. Further, there is no indication that any other churches in the New Testament engaged in this practice.

All this leads to my point. When you say that you want to be like the New Testament church, my response is, which one? Do you want to be like the church in Jerusalem or the church in Ephesus? How about the church in Corinth? Don't forget about the churches (yes, plural) in Galatia. Which New Testament church do you want to be like?

I sometimes hear this line of thinking used when discussing the use of instrumental music in church services. "We shouldn't use instruments in worship because the New Testament church didn't use instruments." First, how do we know? Second, I can see how if you are meeting illegally and in secret (as they did in Rome) that you might not want to blast away on a trumpet. You might instead prefer to sing quietly in a-cappella. That is a practice dictated by the culture and the times, not by the Bible. Third, we shouldn't disregard the Jewish heritage of our Christian roots. In the Old Testament we see extensive use of instrumentation in the Temple to worship God. The use of these instruments was dictated by God Himself. Finally, I don't see air conditioning, water fountains, and toilets in the Bible either, but I have not met too many Christians who think the church should abandon these pagan elements.

There is one thing I have noticed about these churches that they all share in common; they all had problems. Serious problems, which is why Paul was writing to them. Be very careful when you say that we shouldn't do or have something in our churches today because they didn't have it in the New Testament.

Theology versus Methodology

Too many times, I think that Christians get theology mixed up with methodology when it comes to how they think church should be or what they think a church should do. Put very simply, theology never changes, but methodology constantly changes. The Bible is prescriptive when it comes to what our theology should be, and it is descriptive when it comes to the methodology of the early church. In short, what you believe as a Christian and a church stays the same, but how you express and live out that belief is defined by the culture you live in.

Think of foreign missions. When we send a missionary to another country to spread the gospel, that gospel message is the same as the one preached in this country, and the same as the one preached in the New Testament. The goal is the same across cultures and time: to build a church of believers in Christ. Why? Because that's what Jesus told us to do. It is the Great Commission. The church is God's number one instrument to change this world and to usher in the Kingdom of God.

A foreign missionary would never take with him a set of construction plans from this country and attempt to build an "American" church building. That would be absurd. First of all, the church is people, not a building, just as we have established previously. Further, if you ever did build a building for the new church plant, it would look nothing like the buildings in our country. It may not have a steeple. It may not even have a floor other than dirt. Their pews might actually be wooden benches, or the people might even sit on the floor if that is their custom. You see, the methods for building and growing this church of people would be dictated by the culture, but the theology would be dictated by the Bible.

In some cultures the art of storytelling still flourishes. People love to see another person stand up and tell a long epic-type story over the course of hours and even days. That's their custom. Understanding that, the missionary then takes the message of the Bible and begins to tell the greatest Story of all! It's not the way we do it in this country, and it may not be the way it is described in the New Testament, but that does not mean it is wrong. Do I think it is okay to take their pagan practice of storytelling and use it to tell them the Story of God? Yes! Most people have no problem understanding and even agreeing with what I am saying when we put it in the context of a foreign mission experience. For some reason, we do not apply this to the church in America.

There are all kinds of ways to *do* church. Some guys preach in a suit, some guys (like myself) don't even wear a tie. Some guys I know preach in jeans and flip-flops! Some churches use a band and some churches use a choir and orchestra. Some churches own a lot of property and some churches meet in homes and own no property. Which one is better? Neither. They are all the Church, living out their faith, the unchanging faith, as a church in their local community. Rick Warren says that it takes all kinds of churches to reach all kinds of people. When he says that, he is talking about methodology, not theology.

What does all this mean for you? It means you need to find a church that does church the way you are comfortable with and can support. If you don't like the way some church does church, get over it. Don't criticize them. Don't slam them. Don't run them into the ground in your Sunday School class. Pray for them and encourage the members of that church that you may know personally. Aren't we all on the same team?

The Bod(y)

About a year ago a great guy named Johnny Roberts wanted to eat lunch with me. He is a former member of our church, but had left years ago and joined another church in town. But Johnny doesn't live in our town. In fact, he doesn't even live in our state. He lives across the river in Oklahoma in a community called Roland. Sounds like a long way off but it's really only about a 12 minute drive from our church. Johnny wanted to meet with me because he was feeling like God was calling him to plant a church in his home town of Roland where he is a pharmacist. He wanted to know what I thought. We talked and had a great time and I hope I was able to encourage him. I basically said "go for it" and then we just talked strategy.

Johnny had a great vision and so he, along with a good group of people, launched *theBOD.tv*. Kind of an unusual name for a church, huh? Not very New Testament-ish, is it? He also partnered with Life Church in Oklahoma which means that while Johnny is the lead pastor, they receive their preaching and teaching via video from Craig Groeschel. Just about everything related to this new church plant of Johnny's is unconventional. But let me tell you what is not unconventional, his theology. Johnny is a born-again believer of Jesus Christ. He loves God, His Son, and the Holy Spirit. Johnny also loves the Church and he loves people. He especially loves the people of his town. His theology is right on. He planted a new church to reach *new* people. The result? Last I heard, theBod.tv had just under 300 people coming on a weekly basis. Not bad for the first 12 months.

I posted on Johnny's blog back when he was launching, wishing him the best and telling him I'd be praying for him. What breaks my heart is that I know there are other Christians that in their hearts wish him failure. They don't like his methods. Nobody can accuse him of being a heretic, but they just don't like the way he does church. Honestly, I just don't know where that comes from. Is it threatening for people in one church to see success in another church just down the road? Are we really competing against one another? I hope and pray that theBod.tv reaches a segment of people that my church just can't reach. Just as much, I hope that the church down the road that uses an organ every Sunday will reach people that my church just can't reach. I also cry out to God and pray that my church is square in the middle of His will and that we are successful in reaching people that no other church in town can reach.

May we be one Church...

and many churches...

reaching the multitudes...

with the unchanging Gospel.

Chapter 10 – Eternal

We have come to the last chapter. This has been quite a journey. Very personal. This has been, after all, a book about you. You were created to be the Image of God, but that image became severely disfigured. Sin entered into the DNA of mankind. That means that just like you have bones, and flesh and blood, you also have sin. You are a sinner. It means that you are lost, hungry and alone. It means that you are a pawn in this awful game that Satan is playing against God. But it is no game to God. He loves you. He always has. He created you for Himself and He is not willing to give up on what He started. If God created, then He can re-create. He sent His Son, who chose you. The Son chose to save you, to restore that which was lost, the Image of God. That makes you a saint! It means that you are holy because God is holy. You look like Him now. You have been re-created in His likeness. You share many of God's attributes. You are a creator because God is a creator. You are a forgiver because God forgives. It means that the Image of God is not singular but plural, a community. A Body. A Church and a church.

This is the story that has been told in this book. It is the story that the Bible tells in much more detail and richness than I have written about here. I have only touched on what it means to be the Image of God. You may even be thinking now of other ways that we look like God. Volumes more could certainly be written.

Before I close, I want to talk about one more way in which we are the Image of God, created in His likeness. This is perhaps the most important way in which He has made us like Him.

Forever

God is eternal. Have you ever stopped and just dwelt on that concept? If you have, you can't stay there very long because it will start to make your brain hurt. If you think I'm kidding, just try it. I admit now that what I am attempting to write about in the following pages is far beyond my pay grade. I am speaking in the next pages about things of which my knowledge is limited. But I am convinced that even a limited understanding of the eternality of God will help us live and love life in the here and now.

Before the Beginning…

The Bible begins with these words, "In the beginning God…." That tells me that everything that we know — earth, space, stars — all that the Hubble space telescope can see (and even the things it can't see) has a beginning. It means that there was a time when those things didn't exist. In the beginning there was *only* God. Then He created.

It also means that there was a time when there was no *time*. Don't move too quickly past that last statement. Let it sink in. Dwell on it. This is hard for me to grasp because my whole life is dictated by the clock and the calendar. Everything I do has a beginning and an end based on what time it is. I got up at a certain time this morning. I set my alarm so I wouldn't oversleep. School began at a certain time for my kids and I had to make sure they got there…on time. I have a lunch appointment today at a specific time. In fact, I eat almost all my meals based on what time it is. I have appointments today that begin and end by the clock. When I get home tonight, I will check the TV guide to see what time the programming comes on that I want to watch. I will even go to bed at a certain time. That's my life. Driven by the ticking of the clock, the flipping of the calendar, the changing of the seasons. It's probably your life too.

The Bible tells us that there was a beginning to all this. That means there was a time before times. Before the beginning. It means that God has always been there even before there was a "there." Then God decided to create. We tend to focus on the creation of God in terms of the physical dimensions, the things we can see and touch. But God also created the non-physical. God created time itself. God can do that because God is eternal. He is above and outside of time.

The God of Time

There have been some in Christian circles who have, in recent days, claimed that God is not outside of time, that He in fact experiences time linearly just like you and me. This thinking has contributed to the development of openness theology which has as its proponents men such as Greg Boyd, John Sanders, and Clark Pinnock. The idea is that since God experiences time like we do, He does not know with certainty the future. Openness theology is quick to assert that God is omnipotent and is able to shape the future as He desires.

The whole concept of whether or not God is confined to the timeline in the same way we are is critical. The open theist claims that the idea that God is outside of time is not a Hebrew concept, but is a Greek concept that has contaminated Christian doctrine. Openness theology seeks to set this right.

But the Bible, especially the Old Testament, asserts a God who is the Lord over time itself, and thus operates above and outside the timeline. Consider this promise of God in the book of Isaiah. God had just declared that he would deliver King Hezekiah and the city of Jerusalem out of the hand of the King of Assyria. As a sign that this promise would come to pass, God defied the laws of creation and time itself,

"Behold, I will make the shadow cast by the declining sun on the dial of Ahaz turn back ten steps." So the sun turned back on the dial the ten steps by which it had declined.[1]

This is more than a mere setting of the watch back by a few minutes or even an hour such as we do each year for Daylight Savings Time. No, God turned back time itself. The shadow that was cast by the sun declined backward. How is this possible? God. He is above and outside of his creation, that includes time as well.

Consider what has become known as Joshua's Long Day. A day when God got involved with the clock. War has always been with us and will always be with us. Today, battles are fought 24/7. Technology has made nighttime fighting an advantage, whereas in the past, battles were fought only during the daylight hours. If you were losing a fight, you prayed for the sun to set so you could retreat and regroup. Perhaps the setting of the sun would save your men and you would live to fight another day.

In the book of Joshua, we see Joshua in battle against a coalition of nations who had invaded the city of Gibeon, an ally to Joshua's and God's people. Joshua came to their rescue and, with the help of God, was leveling a crushing defeat on the enemy. The afternoon sun was setting fast and Joshua was running out of time to finish the job. Under the cover of night, the enemy would either escape or redouble their efforts and attack again. But Joshua understood that time was not a problem for his God.

> *And as they fled before Israel, while they were going down the ascent of Beth-horon, the LORD threw down large stones from heaven on them as far as Azekah, and they died. There were more who died because of the hailstones than the sons of Israel killed with the sword. At that time Joshua spoke to the LORD in the day when the LORD gave the Amorites over to the sons of Israel, and he said in the sight of Israel, "Sun, stand still at Gibeon, and moon, in the Valley of Aijalon." And the sun stood still, and the moon stopped, until the nation took vengeance on their enemies.*
>
> *Is this not written in the Book of Jashar? The sun stopped in the midst of heaven and did not hurry to set for about a whole day. There has been no day like it before or since, when the LORD obeyed the voice of a man, for the LORD fought for Israel.*[2]

I think this historical account makes it clear that not only is God outside the confines of time, but this concept seems to be a very Hebrew way of thinking about God. There have been those who have tried to make the above passage say something it doesn't say, or they have discounted the passage altogether. Their problem is not with what the Bible says, it is with God. If God is God, something like time is just not a problem for Him.

So Where Did God Come From?

I occasionally get this question, usually from children. And while kids are the ones to most readily ask it, all of us think it from time to time. It's really a great question. The problem with answering this question is that it is asked and then answered from a human perspective. Remember, this is God we're talking about.

Imagine for a moment that you have the ability to enter the world of an ant. What if I create some machine that could transform you into the body of an ant, but you could still retain all the knowledge you have as a human being? Then I place you in an ant colony somewhere, and little Tommy, who lives next door to you, comes along one day and smashes your ant hill, sending all the ants scurrying. When all the little ants get back together, you hear the questions flying, "What was *that*?!" How would you ever begin to explain in a way that an ant could understand who or what Tommy is? No matter how hard you might try, they just wouldn't get it. The differences are too vast.

I know, it's a silly analogy, but the point isn't. The differences between us and God are vast. Far more vast than the differences between a human and an ant.

The deck is stacked against us when it comes to answering the question of where God came from. He's God. He has always been God. He has no beginning. In philosophical terms, He is the first mover who Himself is not moved.

The End?

Just as God has no beginning, He has no end. That is what it means to be eternal. Eternity is not something that can be measured by time. Time, by its very definition, is marked by beginnings and endings. There will come a time when time itself will be no more. In eternity, we will have no need for watches. Time is a convention used only in this creation. Eternity, like God, goes on forever and ever. This is the point where you brain can start to hurt. "How long is forever?" is a nonsensical question because "long" denotes that it can be measured by time. Forever is something *beyond* time.

I know that can be confusing. Think about it like this. Think of time as one grain of sand. Think of eternity as the beach with a coast line that stretches as far as you can see in each direction. Even that doesn't do eternity justice, but it's a start.

God, in His own timing and in His own way, will bring time to an end. The book of Revelation gives us a glimpse of this event.

> *Then I saw a great white throne and him who was seated on it. From his presence earth and sky fled away, and no place was found for them. And I saw the dead, great and small, standing before the throne, and books were opened.*[3]

At the end of time, all of creation will disappear. The clock will stop ticking. All that will be left will be God, people, and a throne. And God will judge.

After God judges, He will create again. You see, God is always creating! We are told that He will create a new heaven and a new earth because the old creation will be done away with. This new heaven and new earth will be different in many ways. One way in which it will be different, that is so often overlooked, is that there will not be any measurement of time. In describing the new Jerusalem, which will be the only city on the new earth, the Scripture says,

> *And night will be no more. They will need no light of lamp or sun, for the Lord God will be their light, and they will reign forever and ever.*[4]

You see, there it is. In its most basic terms, how is time measured? By the sun and the moon. By their rising and their setting. In eternity there is no sun, no moon, no night, only day — all the time. As it says, "forever and ever."

You and God and Eternity

This is where you and I get involved in the whole discussion of eternity. God is eternal. That means He has no beginning and no ending. He is. You and I have been created in the Image of God. That means that we are made in His likeness. One way in which we are like God is that we have the image of eternity stamped on us. It is important to understand that we are not God, we are only *like* God. While the image of eternity is stamped on us, that does not mean we are fully eternal.

God has no beginning, but you and I have a definite beginning. There was a time when you and I were not. There was a specific moment when a sperm and an egg merged and poof, there you were! We do not share eternity with God in the sense that He has no beginning and we do. But as the Image of God, we are eternal in the sense that we have no ending. Once that sperm and egg come together to form a human life, the existence of that life is eternal.

This is what separates us from the rest of creation. This is what makes us special. There is something much more than the physical creation of a person going on. A spirit and soul has been created by God. That spirit is now eternal. Notice the above passage from Revelation again. When the physical creation of God is done away with, the only thing from that creation that is left is us. People. No trees, no rivers, no birds, no fish, no dogs or cats (sorry about that one), nothing — except people. Even then, we are not present at God's throne in the same physical sense that you and I enjoy now. When the human body dies, it dies. It decays and blows away. Ashes to ashes. But the spirit remains. John, who wrote Revelation, says he saw the dead, great and small, standing before God. That's *all* of us.

God's Great Plan

That is what it's all about. All of this. God has a plan, a Great Plan, that He has been working since before the beginning. I am asked from time to time why God bothered with creation. If He knew that there would be so much evil and that people would do the things to each other that we do, why did He do it? If He knew that so many people would reject Him, why did He ever bother?

The answer to that question is that God has been up to something. Something bigger and grander than you or I could ever imagine. That "something" involves you. It involves you as the Image of God. What God is up to is so great that it can tolerate the evil of this world. It can tolerate all the rejection that God experiences from those He created. Let me try in my own limited way to pull back the veil to this Great Plan.

God's Great Plan

Before the beginning, God had an idea. It's not altogether accurate to say that God was lonely, because He is a Trinity. But on some level, God was lonely in that He had so much love and He wanted to share that love with someone. God is love, after all.[5] God's idea involved a Bride. There is no greater picture of love than that of a Groom and a Bride coming together in perfect unity.

Out of this idea for a Bride, God created. He created all that you and I know. He created us. In the beginning that creation started with just one. His name was Adam. The name Adam means "the man." Pretty appropriate, huh? As God looked at His creation, He saw one thing that was not good. He said that it was not good that the man should be alone. God knows something about loneliness because He is, after all, looking for a Bride. He also knows that two are better than one, and that a cord of three strands is not easily broken.[6] *God is Trinity.*

How did God solve this loneliness problem for man? Well, in the same way that God created all that is, from out of Himself, God caused the man to fall asleep and He opened him up. Out of the man, God created woman. The name "woman" means "out of man." Imagine that. Adams's bride was created from out of Adam himself. In his image and likeness, but different, with freewill, just as the man had freewill, just as God has freewill. Freewill is important because love isn't love unless it is freely chosen.

There they were in the Garden of Eden. A trinity. The man, the woman, and God. In perfect fellowship and unity. Then tragedy struck. The freewill of the woman led her away from her husband. Or perhaps it was the freewill of the husband that led him away from his bride. We may never know for sure, but in their freewill, they chose self over each other, and over God. The Bride became a harlot seeking love and satisfaction from another.

This became the story of God's creation. The Great Plan was in jeopardy. But God is a creator and a forgiver. He decided to start again. This time with one man and his family. A man named Noah. God destroyed all freewill life – human life — except for this lone man and his family who found favor in God's eyes. They were the best of humanity. The best portion of his Bride. But even that was not sufficient to eradicate the disease that had infected mankind. That's what it is, a disease. That act of choosing self over others and over God spread throughout all of mankind. Even a flood could not wash it away.

In order to salvage His Great Plan, God decided that He must become involved on a more intimate level. He must raise up His Bride from the ashes of this disaster. So God made a choice. He chose one man. Not a man like Adam, starting perfect and unblemished. This time He started with a man who was thoroughly tarnished. A man who's only hope was God. This man's name was Abram. The name Abram means "high father." But God was not choosing just a man, He was choosing a people, a nation, that would become His people and His nation. Abram would become the father of God's people, a special group of people that God would work through, to whom He would teach and would show His ways.

God gave Abram a promise. He promised that one day Abram's descendants would number the stars in the sky. Because of this, God would create a new name for Abram. He would call him Abraham, which means "father of many." Even in this we see a glimpse of God's Great Plan shining through, for God also made it clear to Abraham that He had not chosen him just to choose him. Oh no, God had chosen Abraham so that through him He might one day bless the whole world.[7]

God's Great Plan began to rise anew. Abraham would indeed go on to have many descendants. As a people, God gave them a name: Israel. Israel means "to struggle with God." It's a very descriptive name because relationships can be like that. A struggle. Remember, God is looking for His Bride. Have you even known a married couple not to fight?

And fight against God these people did. In fact, most of their history is one of fighting against the will of God. They acted like a fickle girlfriend. One day she loves you and the next day she loves someone else. But God is patient, and loving, and forgiving. He is also jealous and possessive of what is His. He chastened and disciplined this people of His. All the while God was planning for something more, something bigger. That's the thing about God, He is always up to something more.

That *"something" involved part of God Himself, a part of His Trinity. It involved His only Son. That "something" would also involve a war, a sacrifice, and a victory.*

When the time was just right, and when God had done all He could do through this people of His, He was ready for His next move in the Great Plan. In perhaps God's most miraculous creative act of all, He sent His Son to this earth in the form of a baby. A common virgin girl of a common Israeli family was found pregnant. That's right, a virgin. But what grew in her was the God-man. God in flesh. Flesh that is God. The God-man was born and given a name, Jesus. It was a common name in that time. A name like John Smith. A common name for the child of a common Jewish girl who lived in a common Jewish town. But this Jesus was far from common and soon everyone would know. They would know that God was on the move. That He had come to visit. That God had come to claim what was His, to work His Great Plan.

Some people got it. But most didn't. Most people were caught up in that disease called sin where everyone thinks it's all about them instead of it being about Him. Even God's own people didn't get it. As a nation, they thought it was all about them. But God was coming because He so loved the whole world. His people had been just a catalyst to bless the world and to work His Great Plan of finding a Bride.

A war was fought. Jesus led the charge. He fought against the disease of self. He fought against sin. He fought against Satan, God's nemesis, the one behind all attempts to destroy the Great Plan. In all wars, sacrifices must be made and God knows this. In fact, this too was part of the Great Plan. The plan to lay down His own Son for the sake of the Bride. You see, the Bride must be pure. That's why brides wear white on their wedding day. It's a symbol of the pure love they are holding for the groom. But God's creation is far from pure. So Jesus was the sacrifice. He died so that the

Bride could live. So that she could be free from disease and be made pure.

I'll be honest, at this point in the story, it seems like God's Great Plan was a failure. The lowest point in creation's history is the point at which the disease of sin appears to win. Jesus died. Killed by those he came to save. Rejected by the one he loves.

But...

Remember, I told you that with God, there is always more!

On the third day after Jesus' death, just long enough for everyone to know that he was dead and gone, Jesus defied death and came back to life! You heard me, a dead man came back to life. But not just any man, the God-man.

And there you have the victory. The disease is defeated. Death's sting is erased. The door is open for anyone to come to God. When I say anyone, I mean anyone. Not just those children of Abraham, but all the children of Adam. Abraham and his descendants had served their purpose, to bring a blessing to the whole world.

At this point the Great Plan involves you. It involves me. It involves my children and my neighbor and the guy that just cut me off on the highway. It involves us all. For you see, we are the Bride of Christ! Because of Jesus, we can be made clean and pure. We can don the white robe and await the wedding day.

But there is a catch...

We have to choose Jesus. He has done his part, but we have to do our part. We must choose to either join God's Great Plan or reject Him. Sadly, God predicts that most will reject Him. They will choose loneliness over companionship. In the end, God will give them exactly what they wish for. An eternity of separation with no hope of relationship.

It is not good that man should be alone. Believe me, God knows. He has come for you, His Bride. He is waiting at the *altar for you. If you choose Him, He will seal you and keep you and when the time is right, come to get you and take you home.*

That, my friend, is the Great Plan of God.

The End of Creation

When God's Great Plan is finished, creation will pass away. Like a cocoon whose only purpose is to house and change that which is within it, creation will fall away like an old husk. That includes your physical body as well. Your body is a product of creation and is subject to the limitations and the laws of creation. As I have already talked about, who you are is so much more than a physical body of flesh and bones. At your essence you are eternal. We all are. We will all continue to live for all eternity.

Those who accept Christ and become a part of his Bride will become residents of a new creation and will enjoy eternal life. Those who reject Christ and refuse to join the wedding party will be separated from this eternal life and instead will endure eternal death.

I take no joy in writing about this, but it is necessary. It is important that you understand what is at stake. There is a literal hell. It is the eternal holding place for the souls of all who reject God's Great Plan. My friend, you have been made by God in the Image of God. That means that while you may have a definite beginning point, there will be no end to you. You will live forever, or perhaps I should say exist, because hell is no way to live. You are eternal.

Annihilation

This is such a hard concept to accept that some people have chosen to reject this clear teaching of the Bible. They have, instead, opted for the doctrine of annihilationism. The annihilationist believes that when creation ends and Christ comes for his Bride, those who have rejected him will not go to hell for all eternity but will instead be annihilated. In other words, just cease to exist.

As the doctrine of hell has become increasingly unpopular to talk about, this doctrine of annihilationism has grown in popularity, even among "orthodox" Christians. Influential theologians such as Clark Pinnock and John R.W. Stott have proposed annihilationism as a more desirable outcome than an eternal hell.

The argument for annihilationism is one seemingly built on human reason rather than Scripture. Proponents just can't fathom that a loving God would sustain a hell with the souls of people being tortured for all eternity. They claim this violates the character of God. There is also the argument made that as long as souls exist who reject God, sin has not been fully defeated. It still exists, just in hell. Only annihilationism grants God a total victory.

The glaring problem with the doctrine of annihilationism is that it violates everything the Bible says about hell and the nature of eternity. Hell is consistently described as eternal. We are told that the smoke of hell goes up forever and ever.[8] Even Jesus, in his own words, describes the punishment of those who reject him as eternal.[9] To be clear, it is appointed for man to live and to die once, and then eternity begins. And eternity is *forever*.

Eternal Perspectives

I have found that living my life with eternity in mind has changed everything for me. I mean everything. I am no longer a prisoner to circumstance. I no longer face defeat no matter what may come.

I shared in the pages of this book the story of my wife who was diagnosed with cancer the first year of our marriage.

To date, she is 15 years cancer free. But it is always in the back of our minds that it could come back. From a temporal standpoint this could be terrifying, even paralyzing. But from an eternal perspective we are free. If the cancer were to return and I were to lose my beloved, I have really not lost her at all. Because of Christ, death is not the end, it is just a change of address. I will see my Julie again. In fact, we have all of eternity to which to look forward. Any separation we may experience in this creation will feel only like a weekend getaway 5,000 years into eternity. This is the gift of God that He has for His Bride.

Eternal perspective is essential for the Christian. It allows you to send your five-year-old to kindergarten on the first day of school and to know that it will be okay. In the same way, you can send your son to Iraq or Afghanistan or wherever our next war is, and know that you will see him again. It enables you to face a heart attack, or Alzheimer's, or financial failure with the hope of a real future.

I hurt for those who do not know Jesus. For the person who rejects him or for the atheist, they are daily held slave to the cruel winds of creation. This life, this world, is all they have.

From an eternal perspective, my life on earth is as close to hell as I will ever be. But to the lost, hungry and alone, to the sinner who is nothing more than Satan's pawn, this life on earth is the only taste of heaven they will ever know. They have topped out. This is as good as it will ever be. And eternity is a long time....

As I bring a close to this chapter and to the words of this book, a book that is about you, I want to defer to the words of C.S. Lewis. I have already stated my affinity for Lewis and his writings. Besides *Mere Christianity*, my favorite collection of his would have to be *The Chronicles of Narnia*. Who doesn't love the tales of Peter, Susan, Edmond and Lucy in the magical land of Narnia? But these were not just mere children's fables. Lewis had a way of weaving deep spiritual truth into the fabric of fiction.

The concluding book in the *Chronicles* series is *The Last Battle*. While I will not spoil the story for you, the ending of that book is the perfect way to end this book. In the final pages, the children come to learn that they have been killed in a railway accident back in the "real" world. Aslan, the lion God-figure of the stories, clears their confusion by reorienting them to an eternal perspective.

And so, my friends, I give you these words of Lewis as a final gift, as has been this whole book. Thanks for reading and if we never meet in this creation, I will look forward to meeting you in the next...

> *"There was a real railway accident," said Aslan softly. "Your father and mother and all of you are – as you used to call it in the Shadow-Lands – dead. The term is over: the holidays have begun. The dream is ended: this is the morning."*
>
> *And as He spoke he no longer looked to them as a lion; but the things that began to happen after that were so great and beautiful that I cannot write them. And for us this is the end of all the stories, and we can most truly say that they lived happily ever after. But for them it was only the beginning of the real story. All their life in this world and all their adventures in Narnia had only been the cover and the title page: now at last they were beginning Chapter One of the Great Story, which no one on earth has read: which goes on forever: in which every chapter is better than the one before.[10]*

Endnotes

Chapter 1 –
1. Genesis 3:1
2. Isaiah 14:12-15
3. John Mintz. "U.S. Called Unprepared for Nuclear Terrorism," *Washington Post*, May, 3, 2005.
4. Graham Allison. *Nuclear Terrorism: The Ultimate Preventable Catastrophe* (New York: Times Books, 2004).
5. Romans 5:12

Chapter 2 –
1. Genesis 3:22
2. C.S. Lewis. *Mere Christianity* (New York: Collier Books, 1960).

Chapter 3 –
1. Centers for Disease Control and Prevention. http://www.cdc.gov/nccdphp/dnpa/obesity/
2. International Herald Tribune. June 19, 2006. http://www.iht.com/articles/2006/06/18/business/ibrief.php
3. Mark 12:30, Luke 10:27
4. Craig Blomberg. *The New American Commentary: Matthew* (Nashville, Tennessee: Broadman Press, 1992).

5. Roger Dobson. "Brian Beats All Computer." *Brain and Mind Journal.* September 14, 2003.
6. 2 Kings 23:25
7. 2 Kings 23:21-23

Chapter 4 –
1. www.seti.org
2. Paul Davies. *Are We Alone?* (London: Penguin, 1995), p. 84.
3. David Wilkinson. *Alone In the Universe? Aliens, the X-Files & God* (Downers Grove, Illinois: Intervarsity Press, 1997), p. 61, 68
4. Ibid. p. 79
5. Genesis 2:18
6. Max Lucado. *Just Like Jesus* (Nashville, TN: Thomas Nelson, 2000).
7. Romans 6:15

Chapter 5 –
1. Luke 22:31
2. Job 1:6-12
3. 1 Peter 5:8
4. Job 1:21-22
5. James 1:12

Chapter 6 –
1. Louis Pojman. *Classics of Philosophy.* (Oxford University Press: New York, 1998), p. 393.
2. A.A. Bevan. "Manichaeism". *Encyclopaedia of Religion and Ethics, Volume VIII* (Ed. James Hastings: London, 1930).
3. *Encyclopedia Americana*, v.2, (Danbury, CT: Grolier Incorporated, 1997), p. 685.
4. Romans 13:13-14
5. Augustine. *Confessions.* Book 5, Section 10.

6. Pojman.
7. http://www.merriam-webster.com/dictionary/saint Accessed on May 3, 2008.
8. http://www.slate.com/id/2090198/ Accessed on June 12, 2008.
9. www.catholic.com. Accessed on June 12, 2008.
10. Romans 8:29
11. Philippians 4:21-22
12. Revelation 3:19
13. Romans 6:6 (New King James Version)
14. 2 Corinthians 5:17
15. Miller, Calvin. *Walking With Saints: Through the Best and Worst Times of Our Lives.* (Thomas Nelson Publishers: Nashville, 1995), p. xxi.
16. Ephesians 4:22 (New King James Version)
17. Luke 9:23
18. Colossians 3:8-10 (New King James Version)
19. Ephesians 2:13

Chapter 7 –
1. Genesis 9:6
2. Retrieved from http://www.abortionno.org/Resources/fastfacts.html on July 24, 2008.
3. Summit Ministries. *Understanding the Times Curriculum: The Case Against Abortion* by Scott Klusendrof. Manitou Springs, Colorado.
4. Romans 1:30
5. Philippians 4:8
6. Ed Young. *The Creative Leader: Unleashing the Power of Your Creative Potential* (Nashville: Broadman & Holman Publishers, 2006), p. 13.
7. Marlene D. LeFever. *Creative Teaching Methods: Be an Effective Christian Teacher*, rev ed. (Colorado Springs: Cook Communication, 1996), p. 46-47.

8. Dr. Laura Schlessinger and Rabbi Stewart Vogel. *The Ten Commandments: The Significance of God's Law in Everyday Life*. (New York: Cliff Street Books, 1998), p. 95.

9. Genesis 2:1-3

10. Exodus 20:8-11

11. Rabbi Joseph Telushkin. *Jewish Literacy*. (New York: William Morrow and Company, Inc., 2008), p. 147.

12. Schlessinger and Vogel, p. 105-106.

Chapter 8 –

1. Matthew 6:9-11

2. This true story of Gary is drawn from Dan Kimball's excellent book, *They Like Jesus But Not the Church*. (Grand Rapids, Michigan: Zondervan, 2007), p. 99.

3. Mark 12:29-31

4. You can read the story for yourself in Matthew 18:23-35

5. Luke 10:25-37

6. The account of Ernest Gordon's life in this chapter is drawn from his excellent book, *To End All Wars*. (Grand Rapids, Michigan: Zondervan, 2002).

Chapter 9 –

1. Hebrews 12:1

2. Matthew 18:20

3. Matthew 10:26-33

4. Hebrews 10:24-25

5. Revelation 1:12-16

6. For a detailed breakdown of the "pagan" claims directed at the institution of the church, see Frank Viola and George Barna's book, *Pagan Christianity?* (Carol Stream, Illinois: BarnaBooks, 2008).

Chapter 10 –
1. Isaiah 38:8
2. Joshua 10:11-14
3. Revelation 20:11-12
4. Revelation 22:5
5. 1 John 4:8, 16
6. Ecclesiastes 4:12
7. Genesis 12:2-3
8. Revelation 20:10
9. Matthew 25:46
10. C.S. Lewis. *The Last Battle* (New York: Collier Books, 1970), p. 183-4.

CPSIA information can be obtained at www.ICGtesting.com
Printed in the USA
LVOW132003050513

332256LV00002B/2/P